Birding Against All Odds

Joan Easton Lentz

Birding Against All Odds
by Joan Easton Lentz

Copyright © 2022 by Joan Easton Lentz
Printed in the United States of America.
September 2022

ISBN: 978-0-929702-14-8

Mission Creek Studios
Santa Barbara, CA
www.missioncreek.com

Design and Layout, Anna Lafferty, Lafferty Design Plus
Copy Editor - Kathy Jean Schultz
Credits:
Front Cover Image - Wanda Alonzo

Back Cover Images:
    Top - Nanette Tobin
    Bottom - Jennifer Lentz

*This book is dedicated to
my daughter Jenny*

Table of Contents

Introduction

2020: A Book Published, A Journey Begun

By June of 2020, I knew it was going to happen: a book I'd been working on for years would be published, and I would live to see it. That book carried my hopes and dreams, and I was ready for it to fly at last.

I wrote it because my life suddenly seemed worth explaining. The threat of dying had put a gun in my back, pushed me over the cliff into action. I wanted the world to know how birds and the natural world had always figured as a major influence in my life, and why. I wanted to piggyback my desire for recovery from a deadly lung disease I'd contracted onto a memoir of how my life used to be.

Filling the pages with the active life of a birder helped me forget about my stunted existence at home. My journals lay open beside me as I wrote, testimony to another life and another person.

I had to explain how it happened.

My message is that nature is a healer and observing how it works is crucial to every stage of human life. Watching birds is one of the ways to understand the natural world. By filling the day with moments of being in nature, benefits compound. It is a way of healing that gives me solace and has allowed me to survive unheard-of challenges.

Lung disease promotes anxiety. Anyone who's held their breath underwater knows what it's like when finally coming up for air. That gasping, shortness-of-breath urgency is with me every moment. And the anticipation of air not being there floods my system with worry. If I am breathing fast due to anxiety, oxygen cannot access the bloodstream the way it should. Therefore, staying calm is a priority.

I learned through the weeks and months of trying to live a meaningful life while I managed my illness that writing was relaxing for me. While writing, I let go of anxiety. I immersed myself in the particular birding adventure I was describing. I was living through the pages of my journals. My lifesaver was a three-ringed binder with lined notepaper. So be it.

I continue to get out birding whenever I can. I have oxygen tanks in various sizes, and I depend upon them every minute of every day. Yes, it's time-consuming, a huge effort, and I am exhausted after a short morning.

Planning a birdwatching excursion is more of a challenge than ever before, but every time I do so, I feel new energy seeping back into me.

I am no stranger to catastrophe. First it was wildfire and mudslide here in Montecito. Then suddenly, two years ago, this virus went on a rampage inside my own lungs. Gasping for breath, and breathing in the whoosh of oxygen from a big machine, I lay in a hospital bed for three weeks. Finally, my body said, okay, I have to get out of here.

I fought back with all that I could muster.

After I was released from the hospital, I struggled to carve out a normal life. I was determined to get better, even though I knew I'd be on supplemental oxygen for the duration.

That first year was a delight, because I was so close to being 100 percent. I had a little oxygen tank on a trolley, but it wasn't heavy and I could push it around easily. I could even manage at night, without being plugged into the big stationary oxygen machine with the higher flow. Like I am now.

Despite a few doom-filled predictions, doctor's calculations, and my own anguished mind, it's three and a half years later and I'm still here. Still kicking. Still wanting to wring out the beauty from every-thing I see outdoors.

Fortunately I have a couple of wonderful doctors, because I cannot bear to go from one doctor to another.

Looking back over my life, what shocks me is all the time I spent trying to preserve or protect my body, preservation "they" said would fend off old age. Forget it.

The body is going to age, no matter how rigorous our exercise plan or how often we skip dessert. The slate of body functions that we must check annually is a nightmare. For those of us with limited time, it's a waste of that time.

⊱❦⊰

Readers might ask the same question I did. What more can she have to write about?

Another bird book? Really?

My answer is that I sought healing in the only way I knew. Writing.

And the only subject I knew how to write about was birding.

I've got that gun in my back, and I never know when it's going to explode. Every day I walk the line between apprehension and relief. Every day that I can walk a distance on my walker is a great day.

Every day that I can look out on my garden, I see the shrubs blos-soming, watch the commonest birds bathe in my pond, and listen to the mockingbird sing like crazy from the top of the olive tree.

At night, I do the crossword puzzle with my husband, Gib, sip a glass of wine, and have a delicious dinner. And sleep. The magic of sleep is never taken for granted at this stage.

But it won't last forever.

Come with me on another wild ride. There's no game plan. And nobody knows where or when it will end.

PART I:
From Younger Days:
Early Adventures

1.

Can Birds Weather The Storm?

Even as a child, I was sensitive to rain, wind, fog, and I loved the sun. Both my parents remarked upon the weather. Just how far had the fog penetrated inland? What time did the sun come out this morning? When's the next storm due? At the time, I thought it was something old people talked about. But I was present and I was listening. Spending time outdoors, as I did every day, I couldn't help but feel the subtle changes in the weather.

In arid Santa Barbara, rain is critical. Without it, nature's normal cycle is broken. All flora and fauna depend upon a certain amount of rain to start the new year. If the ground cover is growing, then the small rodents at the base of the food chain will have food for their young. And these in turn will serve as prey for the bigger birds, and so on up the chain.

I first heard talk of rain at Sunday lunch at my Easton grandparents' home. Their big Dutch Colonial, two-story house was filled with Victorian furniture. Around that mahogany dining room table, which I still have, we'd gather for a rather formal lunch. (That table's had many a Christmas Bird Count organized while sitting around it at my house not so long ago.)

We girls were expected to dress nicely and behave ourselves, while Gertrude, the cook, served us. The food wasn't great, but the discussions about the weather caught my attention.

My grandfather Easton, being a rancher, was big on rain totals. He and Dad talked about the amount of rain that had fallen at the ranch that year, how the grass was coming along, the state of the feed. I was all ears. They spoke of the "filaree," which was the first time I heard this intriguing name. Red Stem Filaree (*Erodium cicutarium)* is the weed that's excellent for forage, and is widespread throughout our pastures.

If winter rains came too early in the fall, the feed would grow up right away and soon wither, if more rain didn't come regularly. Clif Smith, our local botanist, used to say that it wasn't the amount of rainfall, but the spacing of it, that produced a good year for wildflower bloom.

During the last century, I doubt the average citizen of Southern California ever paid much attention to what was going on with the weather. Sunshine! And more sunshine… that's all anybody cared about. Great for surfing, beach-going, and playing outside on 75-degree winter days while our fellow Americans on the East Coast fought cold and shoveled snow.

In contrast, today an awareness of the weather is crucial. Climate change, an accumulation of weather patterns over time, is an ecological phenomenon. Droughts are getting longer and longer. Southern California is always one of the last western regions to pull free from the label of "Severe" or "Extreme" on the Drought Monitor Map. And it will continue to be more extreme. In fact, there is literature that suggests the 20-year drought we've been in since 2000 – excepting a few wet years – is similar to one that threatened several civilizations in the Southwestern states centuries ago.

The National Oceanic and Atmospheric Administration (NOAA) just issued a summary of weather temperatures, over the last 20 years, that deviate from climate normals. Throughout the U.S., we are one degree warmer now compared to two decades ago.

Similarly, meteorologists found that it was wetter in the eastern and central parts of the country, and dryer in the west, compared to the average of 1971-2000. In order to rule out weather variations, NOAA looks at 30 years of data for comparison for both the wet and dry measurements for climate change.

Once I understood that learning about birds meant more than just identifying them, I realized the influence of weather. And the first aspect that grabbed me was rainfall. I began recording precipitation at our house here in Montecito. By recording rain totals year after year, I found my numbers came remarkably close to other official rain measuring sites.

The first of what was later to be called a "March Miracle," occurred in late February-March of 1991. It was a drought-buster series of storms. The high-pressure system that had been blocking storms from Alaska moved off, enabling wonderful rain to wash down our California coast.

After the March Miracles in the early 1990s, the year 1995 turned up two "100-year flood" events. On two occasions — January 10 and March 19 — storms dumped heavy rain on the south coast.

And then there was the grand finale. The El Nino of fall-winter 1997-98 was our wettest year on the record books.

At the time, I recall reading in various references that the 2000s were predicted to be a dry cycle. This is the influence of complicated climate phenomena thousands of miles away from here, also known as the Pacific Decadal Oscillation. Add climate change and the effects of human activity, and you have the generally warmer "dry 2000s."

But in the winter of 1998, I was there at the biggest rainfall season that ever occurred in Santa Barbara County. At the time, we weren't sure what was happening, but we knew it was important. I was anxious to describe my personal El Nino storm story, so I wrote this in my journal:

Nature Journal: January 18, 1998
Racing A Storm Down California

Gib and I plan to walk out along the cliffs by the Presidio, before driving south to Santa Barbara. We've been staying in San Francisco, and I want to see what a big storm gathering offshore looks like.

We hike south from the Seacliff area along a muddy

path. Dark crags plunge to the surf below. Cypresses
cling green and wet beside the trail. We look back
over our shoulders to the Golden Gate Bridge. Not a
boat in sight.

I scan west out over an angry ocean.

There it sits on its haunches, a beast of a storm,
a frightening bank of dark clouds to the west,
positioned, waiting. In layer after layer of gray bands
above the horizon, as far as I can see, the storm
clouds build.
The wind blows from all directions, strewing white-
caps over the ocean.

A few raindrops plop down. It's time to go.

We're sure we can out-drive this storm on our way
south, pulling just ahead of it every bit of the journey.

By noon we are at 19th Street going south on
Highway 1. Sheets of rain pummel the car. We
can't see the car ahead of us, can't make out the
lane lines, creep along through inches of water.

Slowly, as we crawl forward, a mist lifts and a fog
forms. The rain retreats. We've outrun the storm
for the moment.

But clouds race to overtake us. Once on the 101,
we hit scattered showers. On either side above the
mountain ranges, we see fragments of blue. Good.

Five minutes later, it begins to pour again.

The Monterey hills are dark and threatening.

Surely, the Salinas Valley will still be dry? It is.

Sun, showers, clouds, and wind. The fierce west wind

pushes and whips, nudging the car off the pavement. eucalyptus trees near the highway send twigs and branches hurtling over the road.

Dodging the tumbleweeds proves worse than the tree branches. Tumbleweeds roll across fields and pastures, pile up in the corners of fences. Then up and over they go, right onto the highway scooting along the road like macabre wild animals. Cars brake and twist to avoid them.

Way out on the coast the mountains are enveloped in rain, but not here. We're headed southeast, and could this be like so many "drought rains" we've had? Will it fizzle out before it gets to Santa Barbara?

We're now nearing Paso Robles. I'm wondering if this is "El Nino" or just a good old-fashioned winter storm. Why is it so warm outside?

As we skim through San Ardo, a pair of Red-tailed Hawks careens wildly over a field. An American Kestrel gives up trying to perch on the power lines, taking cover in a low tree. Turkey Vultures dip and swerve like drunken toys.

At San Luis Obispo, we hit heavy mist and clouds.

We round Gaviota by 5 p.m. Though the sea shows a ruffled chop, the violent wind on land subsides. Dead calm along the Gaviota coast, palm trees slack, quiet.

We arrive home, see enormous clouds over the Santa Ynez Mountains, but no rain at all. Darkness falls. We made it, we've beaten the storm.

And then we hear... that pitter-patter on the tin roof over the back porch. Louder and louder.

Ahhhh… it's begun. We look outside, the deck light is on, and we see the raindrops begin to thicken and speed up. I'm overjoyed. The storm caught up with us at last.

Santa Barbara's average annual precipitation is approximately 18 inches. But rainfall at our Montecito home reached 54.40 inches in that year, 1998.

In downtown Santa Barbara, the wettest year on record was previously 45.25 inches in 1941, but was then broken in 1998 at 46.97 inches, a result of the El Nino year.

Climate Change and Birds

As mentioned above, many years during the 2000s saw unusually low winter rainfall totals. The Drought Monitor Map came into existence, showing us Californians which counties were the driest. Soon the whole state was being included.

The problem is that the natural variation of what we call La Nina (the dry climate phase) has been affected by global climate change. It seems that human-caused tweaking has amplified the natural variations, resulting in more frequent droughts, floods, and fires. In the southwestern states, La Nina brings a dry, rainless winter, whereas along the Eastern seaboard colder, snow-filled days are predicted.

Thousands have fled flooding in Australia, but in the Eastern Horn of Africa prolonged drought threatens to bring famine.

The complexity of climate change, when added to weather cycles, only makes the discussion more complicated. When it comes to birds, we must go slowly and think outside the box. I suspect that each species of bird will have to adapt to climate change in its own way.

Ornithologists noted first that spring migration was taking place earlier than ever before. Birds had begun to flee their winter homes for their summer breeding ranges several days earlier year over year. What does this *phenology* (the relationship between environmental conditions and biological processes) mean for the bird?

If caterpillars of a certain kind hatch at a special time, and the bird who feeds them to its young has already had a nest with nestlings fledged… well, it will miss out on that bit of protein to feed, right?

Thus, the phenology of the caterpillar is not meshing with that of the bird, which will have to be made up for in some way.

Climate change has already begun to affect birds' home ranges and habitats. Throughout the world, and on several continents where it's been measured, scientists are noting that bird species are breeding at higher elevations and further north than they were before.

This is described as a poleward latitudinal shift in ranges, and it means birds are seeking cooler temperatures and more precipitation.

Thus, species that generally have a more southerly origin will do better and will have less of a journey than those that are more northerly-oriented and need a cooler climate.

Thermoregulation in a bird's body is crucial, as is the presence of specific plants and prey items that make up the habitat they live in. With climate influencing the weather – as it does through changes described above – birds may not be getting the food and shelter they require from a suitable home range.

One theory posits that some of the birds we define as off-course vagrants may be adventuresome pioneers searching to colonize a more fruitful area. They are not lost, but rather are leaders. If the birds touch down at a rewarding habitat, they may be at the forefront of a group of their kind.

In 2014, the U. S Environmental Protection Agency (EPA) issued a paper showing changes in the winter ranges of North American birds. Annual change in the latitude of a bird's center of abundance for 305 bird species in North America from 1966-2013 was more than 40 miles. Of the 305 species studied, 62 percent have moved their wintering grounds northward since the 1960s, while 27 percent have shifted southward. Others have not moved at all.

On average, bird species have also moved their wintering grounds farther from the coast since the 1960s. Inland areas tend to experience more extreme cold, but those extremes are less severe as the climate warms.

This indicator study was the result of the National Audubon Society's Christmas Bird Count, which takes place every year in early winter. Although this is a volunteer effort, and errors can be caused by a variety of factors, it's a worthy example of what was occurring even as early as the middle of the 20th century.

One dataset showed that climate change has likely caused migratory birds' bodies to get smaller and their wings to get longer. The study originated at Chicago's Field Museum, and included hundreds of birds that had bumped into windows in the Windy City's buildings. The recorded body size and wing length of every bird measured was included in the calculations.

Over 40 years, bodies generally got smaller and wings got longer. When scientists overlaid this with climate information they found a clear pattern. Periods of rapid warming were followed closely by body size decline.

Using the same data, scientists found that spring migration got earlier by about five days over the years, while the timing of fall migration broadened. The duration of fall migration had stretched out by about 17 days.

I realized from this information that each bird species will respond differently to the question of global warming. It's not simple, and furthermore, there are other organisms involved.

Each species will undergo special conditions. How they react to climate change will depend upon how successful they are in surviving.

But birds are born to survive.

Transition, adaptation, and on they go. Climate change has been happening for some time now. The question is, if the pace picks up, can birds still handle the challenges?

Nature Journal: July 25, 2015
The Silence Of The Drought At Cold Spring Creek

Today was clear, hot. Dry, dry, dry.

As I was walking up Cold Spring Canyon this morning, I thought of the silence that drought brings.

There's no sound in the creeks.

The riparian corridor still stands, the trees like silent sentinels. Except they aren't really silent inside. Inside they're screaming for water, water, water. The alders in particular have taken a hit. Dead alders. Their roots aren't getting the precious moisture needed to make the alders thrive.

Silent canyons. The expectation is to hear water running.

And where are the birds? I hear no Yellow Warblers in June and July this year. Yellow Warblers need riparian habitat. But without water, where are the insects? No Warbling Vireos. No Purple Finches.

Have they gone to higher elevations? Is everything OK at the few perennial streams along the south coast, such as at the upper portions of Arroyo Hondo?

All I know is that drought means silence. Fewer bird songs, mean fewer nesting pairs. Will the birds move north, shifting their range ever so slightly to find better conditions?

I wonder.

But in nature, nothing is forever. Change is just around the corner. We could be flooding in two or three months. Will El Nino deliver its promised rainfall?

Who knows?

Right now, I see the Coast Live Oaks with brown clumps of leaves: they are suffering in silence.

So are the Valley Oaks, so are many of the street trees in Santa Barbara. When I deep-watered the trees in my garden, they pushed out new green tips.

Water. Water in the West.

I love the stark landscapes, the spare vegetation, the striking views, because I'm a Westerner. But this is different. This is pain and suffering, beginning at the lowest level.

So when the rains come, if they ever do, it will not be silent.

But now, the silence of the drought lies on the landscape like a shroud.

2.

Redstart Dreams

As birders, we're consumed by "firsts." The first time we see a bird we've never set eyes on before, we call it "a life bird." The first time we see a bird returning in the spring is a "first" of the season. Or the first time we note the arrival of a winter visitor, we write it down. For those of us who live and work in the area, the first time we see a bird in Santa Barbara County is a very big deal.

This story begins in 1975, when I traveled to Southeast Arizona on a bird trip with my husband. I'd persuaded Gib to spend a vacation looking at birds. Not that he didn't like them, but he was definitely indulging me. I'd read page after page about certain tropical birds from Mexico that overlapped into the U.S. Everybody said it was the most exotic place you could go and still be in the States, at least for birds. Ready to leave in a heartbeat, I was.

It was the kind of adventure I'd had dreams of, but never thought I'd actually do.

We were a young couple with a limited budget, squeezing a driving trip to Arizona into little over a week when it should've been two. Our two children were shipped off to Gib's folks, who were delighted to watch them.

And I was a nervous wreck. Those were the days before bird tour companies had emerged as a way of going birding in a strange place. You were still expected to figure out how to discover these birds by yourself.

A man named James Lane was well-known as the author of pamphlet guides birders could use to find birds throughout the U.S. The "Lane Guides" were filled with exact directions for finding the specialty birds wherever you traveled. They were the earliest of the do-it-yourself birding books, and the descriptions of how to locate bird after bird, complete with mileage and road directions, were tops.

For the Arizona trip, we were instructed to carry a cassette recorder (heavy) in our backpack, on the hike to see the Red-faced Warbler. According to Lane, we might need the recorded sound of the Northern Pygmy-Owl to attract small warblers. This whole concept mystified me, until I realized the mobbing action that such predators put in motion. When I understood that it was a way of luring a bird out that I wanted to see, I could imagine a group of warblers as part of an alarm chorus around the owl.

So I'd packed the suitcases, backpacks, binoculars, books, and maps. Plus the big cooler, and all the other paraphernalia for a road trip.

I worked myself up to a fever pitch, I confess. Either that or I'd caught a bug.

Literally, when we stopped at Blythe, I was running a fever and I felt horrible.

We figured we'd spend one night in this place, and boy did we choose a cheapo.

With its faded green paint, and the room door that didn't close tightly, we got what we'd paid for, a low-end motel.

Here I was on the bird trip of a lifetime and I felt like I had the flu.

Gib went somewhere and brought me back dinner. We tried to go outside to eat, but it was so much cooler in the room, so we stayed put. A rickety cooler in the window furnished the only air conditioning, better than nothing.

We were in T-shirts and shorts and I was shivering and sweating at the same time.

When we went outside to see what was happening around the pool, we noticed a young family that had brought a puppy along. They were staying in the room beside us.

I didn't think anything more of it, until that night, when I awoke all of a sudden.

"Gib, there's an animal in this room!" I wailed. Poor Gib. Exhausted, he sat up looked around, then looked under the bed.

And out popped that puppy that belonged next door.

By this time I was sure I was hallucinating.

Then we both remembered the door to our room that didn't close properly.

In the middle of the night, Gib returned the puppy to the family next door.

Onward through the desert we drove, hitting Tucson on a broiling evening and heading on south to Ramsay Canyon. At that time, it was owned by The Nature Conservancy, and a dozen cabins were available for visitors to stay in. After collapsing into bed and waking up to the cool canyon morning, I crept out barefoot to stare in wonder at my first sight of a Painted Redstart.

There it was. The bird we had driven hundreds of miles to see: the Painted Redstart, a vision of black with a deep crimson breast, white wing bar, and *white crescent under each eye*. The redstart flared its tail and fluttered about in an elegant dance. I could hardly believe my luck, but later I found them commonly, on this trip.

My fever broke. The gorgeous canyon where we stayed, down which a creek flowed, was one of the best birding spots ever. I got many life birds just by walking outside our front door.

Skip forward to 1982, when a Painted Redstart landed in Santa Barbara at Rocky Nook Park out of nowhere, just like the one did this weekend (2021).

By then I'd learned that just because I'd seen a Painted Redstart in Arizona where they *belonged*, that did not count as seeing one in our part of the U.S., where it was considered *rare*.

I knew that a Painted Redstart here in our neck of the woods was worth much more than one in Arizona.

It was a November day in 1982, and I'd just heard there was a Painted Redstart in town.

I was working at Gib's office in the mornings, and I'd had a lunch break with a friend. After lunch, I ran to my car, then headed for a certain lane off Mission Canyon Road. I knew the redstart was on private property, and I was determined to see it before the day was over.

I pulled up to a lovely two-story Victorian house, rang the doorbell, and waited impatiently.

My friend, who was really an acquaintance, slowly opened the door. "Why, Joan, how nice to see you!" she exclaimed.

Then the words came bursting out of me. How I knew she had a rare bird in her garden, how beautiful the bird was, how I was dying to see it.

I even pushed past her into the living room, hoping to find where the back garden was.

"Would you like to see the patio?" she said nervously.

"Yes, yes, that would be fabulous," I replied, breathless.

And she lead the way out another door to a flagstone patio under the oaks.

"There it is!!" I shouted. And that was how I met my first Santa Barbara Painted Redstart, as it climbed and danced its way up an oak tree in my friend's garden.

I rudely drooled while I ogled the bird. My poor friend, she couldn't quite get a grip on me at all.

Nature Journal: December 13, 2021
Rocky Nook Park, Santa Barbara

This latest sighting of mine was very different. I'm now on oxygen 24/7 so I need a tank by me, and a caregiver to trundle it along. I also have a walker to hold onto as I go, and as a place to sit when I get there.

This was all well and good, but the biggest rainstorm of the year threatens to arrive any minute today.

Last night I thought of how difficult it would be to

navigate that path in the mud after a soaking rain,
and I determined I must try to see the redstart
this morning.

As usual, my wondrous caregiver, Jean, was up to
the challenge and ready to go!

Her strength is my secret weapon.

We park in the handicapped parking space at the
north end of the park, and off we trudge. I struggle
and we do some "four-wheeling" as we bump and
shudder over the rocks in the dirt pathway. The incline
of the trail is upward.

It's hard, but I'm doing it. Friendly birders lure me to
the path ahead. They offer to help me find the redstart.

Finally arrived at the spot, I plop down gratefully on
my walker. On the other side of a chain-link fence, a
shaded garden is filled with oak trees. Their gnarled
branches make a thick canopy against the sky.

The skies stay gray and angry today, darkening with
the minutes as I wait.

We sit patiently. I chat with friends.

I am so relieved I've made it I don't care if we miss the
bird or not.

Then one birder points, and another, and then I myself
see that lovely warbler, getting fabulous views.

The poor Painted Redstart is a bit subdued by the cool
weather, so it loiters in its daily ballet from tree to tree
searching for insects.

The grayish-white sky is not providing the best of
backgrounds, but there's no getting over that crimson

chest, the white tail flash, and the dewdrop crescent of white below the eye.

This is a bird you can only dream of until you see it in real life, and even then you have to pinch yourself.

We here in the temperate U.S. have been brought up to look at little brown and white birds with a few tinges of color. The sight of one of these subtropical lovelies is enough to turn you into a holy grail birder, if you aren't one already.

What do I mean by that? You'll go anywhere you can to find a rare bird.

Just like I did. And it began with dreams of seeing a Painted Redstart in 1975.

3.
Birding Cuyama

Back to Santa Barbara County, California, where I picked up my oldest notebook and found these bird jottings from a trip to the Cuyama Valley in 1980. I couldn't wait to put this entry together with some other material I wrote about my sister's property in that same valley.

My First Cuyama Bird Trip:
November 16, 1980

The first bird notes I ever took came about because Paul Lehman and Jon Dunn, both expert birders who lived in Santa Barbara, wanted to explore the remote Cuyama Valley back in the 1980s.

I was an unabashed newbie at the whole idea of taking real field notes. Everything I'd learned about birds had been self-taught. I'd typed notes on 3x5 cards, and I'd filled some notebooks with names of birds and places where I'd found them, but as to proper field notes? What were those?

This whirlwind trip to the Cuyama was a demo of the "sink or swim" method. Not only for birdwatching but for how to take notes.

First off, they told me about the codes birders use when they need to shorten bird names. For a bird with a one-word name, use the first four letters. A Wrentit is a WREN which is confusing, but follows the rule.

Next, for a bird like Spotted Towhee, take the first two letters of the bird's descriptive name followed by the first two letters of the bird's species name. In other words: Spotted Towhee is abbreviated to SPTO.

It gets a little complicated when you have a three-word name, and the first two are hyphenated. Green-winged Teal is GWTE.

Unwieldy at first glance, using the code speeds up the listing process.

Of course, to be authentic, all lists should be in the bird's full English name, since official bird names may change over time, depending upon the current taxonomy.

In the event, we three were driving along in a boxy Honda Civic, and I was supposed to be taking the notes, which I'd never done before.

The trip started in Santa Barbara when I met them at 5 a.m., and ended around 7 p.m. in Santa Maria. By that time I was exhausted, depleted, and thoroughly overwhelmed.

I learned this about taking notes: You stop, and take notes at a certain area of habitat. Don't lump multiple stops of a day's birding all into one list. You move from one general location to another during a day of birding.

You need to estimate *numbers* as well as *species*. Obviously, you'll be most accurate at the lower numbers of birds observed. For higher numbers, count by tens and estimate wisely.

Important or unusual sightings should be underlined or asterisked. The more detail you can include, the better.

In those days, we sketched rough drawings. Now, birders attempt as many photos as they can to bolster their identification of birds. A cellphone can help.

But oh the Cuyama we saw then.

What To Look For

Visiting the Cuyama for the first time is like going to another land, it's that different from the shores of the county's South Coast. The Cuyama Valley lies only 35 miles north of Santa Barbara as the crow flies, but it takes a couple of hours to get there by car.

The sky is big and goes forever. The Sierra Madre Mountains are steep oak and pine woodland on one side of the valley, and the Caliente Mountains are high-desert bare on the other side.

Short-grass fields and pastures stretched for miles down the main valley. There were acres of fallow fields, some with tumbleweeds piled in corners. The scrubby brush on the hillsides came right down to the fields. Blowing dust whirled from the sharp north wind.

Paul Lehman had the whole route mapped out beforehand, because he was already contemplating his "Birds of Santa Barbara County" thesis for UCSB. Nobody had studied the bird life of this area, and it needed to be added to whatever bird knowledge Paul had gathered about the rest of the county.

In accordance with this, we stopped at bleak, deserted-looking farmhouses, where a few tamarisk trees or a cottonwood might encourage a vagrant to pause and rest. We did find two birds: a Townsend's Warbler, and a Varied Thrush, both of which were off-course.

We drove along Foothill Road, then pulled over at the famous dairy feedlot. Here, where cows munched from feed containers, hundreds and hundreds of Tricolored Blackbirds fed, mixed in with Red-winged Blackbirds and European Starlings. Nearby were several farm ponds, where the birds roosted at night.

What's the difference between a Tricolored and a Red-winged Blackbird? The stripe closest to the wing's tip is bright white in a Tri-colored, and yellowish in the more familiar Red-winged Blackbird. Often, one notices the white wing bar before any other mark, since the adjacent red bar on the wing may be covered.

Tricolored Blackbirds are a special California species. Now, due to precipitate drops in the population of this species, the Tricolored Blackbird is proposed to be listed as Threatened, under the Endangered Species Act.

But Jon and Paul weren't looking for Tricolored Blackbirds. They were anxious to get out of the car and walk the grazed fields. Once out stalking, the guys were looking through the Horned Larks and American Pipit flocks in order to find a longspur. I was in awe of the way they could hear the longspur's "rattling" call, if one were to be mixed in with the more common larks and pipits.

Walking through a field of cut alfalfa, you could hear the flocks of Horned Larks. They gave a high "tew-lip" call as they flew over. Horned Larks at a distance look like a brown sparrow with a square black tail. Large groups flew in smooth aggregations, changing direction and always in synch, the way a shorebird flock would be, but flying over fields.

The American Pipit – another field denizen – with another call to commit to memory, was added to the mix. Pipits have an undulating flight, and I never managed to get onto one before it disappeared over the next pasture. It was tough birding.

The total numbers of certain species of birds I have jotted down are high. I know they're correct because Jon and Paul dictated what to write. In the upper Cuyama Valley alone, we saw:

15 American Kestrels
15 Ferruginous Hawks
3,500 Horned Larks
1,000 Mountain Bluebirds
5,000 Tricolored Blackbirds

You won't get numbers half as high as that today. Thankfully, I wrote it all down.

On that trip I got my baptism by fire from these two experts. So much to absorb.

There are many-pronged objectives on an expedition like this. What bird species could be expected to be present? What could you document that was rare or out of place? What should be your method of birding such an area? All these were questions that rode along in the car beside me.

Out came the notebook and pencil. No cellphones, or computers in those days to help me. I found most of my information in books. If expert birders were around, you might get lucky.

Every night when I came home from a day of birding, I tried to make a list of the numbers of birds I'd seen, and what I'd learned about them.

After this day, my head was splitting. I didn't know how to tell a Northern Harrier from a Ferruginous Hawk.

The Merlin we saw was the first I'd ever been shown. This small, dark hawk is a miniature version of a Peregrine Falcon, and just as clever at pursuing birds. The males have a definite "helmet" of dark gray, similar to a Peregrine. We saw one perched in a bare tree. Later we squinted through the spotting scope at the same Merlin far away, as it sat atop a dirt clod plucking a freshly-killed pipit.

I didn't have any background on birds that I hadn't seen locally. It was embarrassing, but I didn't need to apologize. I felt comfortable just sitting there learning what I could.

Ever since that first trip to the Cuyama, I've been drawn to the empty spaces and the chance to explore a wilder landscape.

More Birding in Cuyama Valley

As luck would have it, I had more opportunities to go birding in the Cuyama Valley than I'd ever contemplated on that day back in 1980.

My sister, Ellen Easton, one of my favorite companions for nature expeditions, had gone and done what none of our generation had been able to do – own an interest in a ranch.

Ellen was a person who knew what she wanted and had a way of getting it. I admire that in her. When a parcel of land came up for sale in 2004 in the Cuyama Valley, she and other friends pooled their resources and got together to buy a ranch.

And I, as the resident naturalist, claimed birding rights.

We had fabulous times at that ranch, situated in a canyon just north of the Sierra Madre Mountains. I got to know the pinyon pines of those canyons and the enormous dark green juniper bushes of the flattened arroyos.

Harsh country, her ranch reminded me of what cowboying on the old Sisquoc Ranch might have been like. Annual rainfall is sparse.

Cattle are the main crop, and the years of little feed outnumber the good ones.

The Cuyama Valley is in the rain shadow of two major mountain ranges: the Santa Ynez and the San Rafael. You aren't going to get a heck of a lot of rain pouring into that dry valley up there, although you will have the threat of a flash flood every now and then.

Ellen and her co-owners were good stewards, and the times we botanized and birded all over that ranch are etched in my memory.

Nesting season in early spring was the most exciting.

The big gray barn harbored two large-stick raven nests for many years. Then, the ravens were thrown out of their own homes. When a Great Horned Owl moves in, a raven leaves. That's the way it is with this apex predator, the Great Horned. The owl doesn't mess around constructing nests. Ravens and hawks will build a structure, then abandon it when the owl comes calling.

And the owl now has a nest.

Or, as happened once on the ranch, the owl nested earlier in the season in a Red-tailed's nest, in the lone cottonwood by the entrance gate. When the owls were finished, the Red-tailed Hawk pair arrived to retake the nest and produce their own offspring.

Often, in springtime in the barn, two fierce-looking juvenile Great Horned Owls scowled down at me. With their thick feathers of gray and black, and the two "ear tufts" sticking out above their faces, these youngsters looked close to being adult. They were almost as big, too.

By March, the female Great Horned Owl was not around. Under cover of night, she had been delivering prey to the owlets. Then one day, I found both young owls out of the nest. One was sitting on top of an old ladder. The other had fledged, off to practice night hunting on its own.

I walked all over that property looking for nests. A Say's Phoebe, a little flycatcher that rarely nested in Santa Barbara, was at home here within a snug formation of mud and twigs atop a light fixture on the porch. The female raised a brood of four in these cramped quarters, feeding them endlessly during daylight hours.

The most memorable nest was the one I nearly stepped on. The rains had come down plentifully that year, and a nice mix of grasses and wildflowers covered the ground. I was with my grandson Alex and his cousin, Tyler, boys of nine or ten. They'd been down playing in the wash that doubled as a creek that year. We were all muddy, and it felt good.

As we headed back to the ranch house, I kept hearing the clear, piping melody of a Western Meadowlark song. I saw the meadowlark balancing on a barbed wire fence nearby, bright yellow breast catching the sun.

We kept on walking and talking.

Suddenly both boys pointed at the ground in front of me. I stopped and leaned over to see what was there. A meadowlark's nest, with four pale blue eggs, was covered with a light thatch of grasses. A tunnel, through which the meadowlark parents would travel on their way to and from the nest, was another feature. Forming a camouflaged hallway to the nest, the tunnel enabled the parent birds to feed the young without giving away the nest's location to a predator's eye.

I tried to explain this to the boys, how meadowlarks always nested on the ground, but they were more interested in a horse that had wandered over. I was afraid the horse's hooves would trample the nest, so we quickly walked away.

And the most numerous nester of all? Nowhere to be seen... California Quail.

Thousands of these quail occupy this land. The grasslands and the pinyon/juniper uplands are attractive to this most beautiful of birds. Its subtle black, gray, and white plumage fits in perfectly.

And there the quail are, walking all around at other seasons of the year, but not in springtime.

You may hear their call "Chi-CA-go!" echoing from the hillsides, but all you'll see is the sentry bird, the male watchdog. The females are up hidden on nests. They retreat from the lowlands and march off to their own tunes, to their own natural rhythms.

You can't see them, but they are there. Attending to important egg-laying and brood camouflage chores, parent quail take their jobs seriously.

All at once, come early summer, they'll be down again to the water features, to the grass that's still green around the buildings. The quail subsist mostly on the discarded seeds of saltbush and narrow-leaved daisy, sagebrush and coyote bush.

This journal entry describes a morning's birding at Ellen's ranch.

Nature Journal: November 20, 2004
Cuyama Valley

This morning in damp, cold "tule" fog, Ellen and I go birding.

Walking out from the adobe onto the surrounding pastures, I carry the scope to see what we can find. Tiny shoots of green grass spread out in a carpet; yellow rabbitbrush, a fall bloomer, brightens the edges.

First, we pick out the shape of a Prairie Falcon sitting high on a power pole along the line that runs over the hill. Alone and pale gray, the falcon waits for its opportunity to strafe the morning flocks as they feed in the fields.

Large groups of Lark Sparrows, Mourning Doves, and Brewer's Blackbirds forage in the grasses, their attention fastened on the ground; not too watchful. As I explain about the Prairie Falcon, and tell Ellen of its fondness for doves, how their fast, deep wingbeats mirror the flight of the falcon, we are interrupted.

A gray-brown shape comes roaring low over the fields, sneaking up on the doves, bent on separating one of them out for breakfast. Instantly, the doves explode in a blur of whirring wings and flee.

We watch the Prairie Falcon stoop and strike at one of the doves, but the dove angles sharply and it escapes. Panic ensues. The doves, Horned Larks, and Brewer's Blackbirds speed away thoroughly frightened. Some gather on the fence lines, others disappear.

We're up for a walk, and we can't quit till we've tried for the eagle.

We tramp along down the track.

A Golden Eagle used the area as a winter territory, and we could sometimes see it if we were at the right angle. The eagle liked the top of the ridge, where several rocks gave good look-outs.

At last we reach the place where we could search the ridgelines with our binoculars. I even set up the scope.

Blurry, blurry, can we make that an eagle? Turn the dial just a little, and despite the wind...

There it is far, far away – a big-shouldered silhouette, brown against the gray hillside. We wonder when it will leave or if it will stay up on that windy hill all morning, till it finds suitable prey. Would it settle for a jackrabbit or a pocket gopher? The ground we've walked on is a mass of burrows.

So far away was the eagle, we wondered if we were dreaming. And then we saw a shadow tap the air lightly and soar wide-winged down the side of the hill and off into the next canyon. No mistaking the Golden Eagle. Good hunting, then oh eagle.

PART II:

Life Changes,
And A Pandemic

4.

Collapse

September 2020

I sit out on our back deck, letting the evening light wash over me.
I am in an agony of indecision and fear, have no idea what to do or
where to turn.

Gib, my husband and sole caretaker for the past two years, had
fallen off his bike that morning and broken his leg.

At 8:15 a.m., I watched as he joked with paramedics from the
Montecito Fire Station. I'd just called 9-1-1, and they were at our
house in three minutes.

So swiftly, it all comes apart, doesn't it?

Gib tripped and caught his shoe getting off his bike.

And boom. Our lives changed forever.

With my lung disease, I cannot manage this house alone. And now,
my only helper, Gib, needed help, too.

After talking with the surgeon, Gib called me from the hospital,
and told me his surgery was scheduled for the next day. He had broken
his big leg bone, the femur, and it needed to be mended with the help
of screws and stitches.

I knew he was in terrible pain, and that he had to stay in the hospital for a week before he could come home. Of course, in this pandemic
time, no visitors of any kind were allowed.

And there I sat, not knowing if Gib would need a nurse when he came home, or whether he could manage on a walker or what?

I felt as if there was nobody I could ask about this. Between my state of dependence, and his need for post-op nursing care, weren't we going to require some assistance?

Of course, but what kind?

For days I dialed phone numbers, made notes, got more and more confused. Scribbled notebooks lay everywhere, their pages full of instructions.

My anxiety went off the charts. Doctors wanted me to be on mood elevator pills, but I couldn't tolerate them.

The weather was unbearably hot, as it can be in September, and although we'd signed up to get some air conditioning installed in the bedroom wing of the house, it was delayed.

Our weather cycle involved one heat wave after another that summer. Heavy Santa Ana winds, forest fires up and down the state, day after day of high temperatures. The hot weather drove me crazy.

The oxygen I need is much harder to get on a hot day than a cold one. Oxygen molecules are farther apart in the heat than in the cold. So, on any day above about 80 degrees, the machines I depend upon have a harder time scooping the oxygen out of the air and concentrating it.

What I didn't realize at the time, but is clear in hindsight, is that every medical situation is different. Each one has an individual solution. And the one that I could not foresee is the one that I needed: constant help in the house all the time. Twenty-four/seven, as they say.

Remember, this was Covid time, so we were trapped. Trapped by the threat of infection, trapped by our broken bodies, trapped by an inability to figure out our future at the snap of a finger. Just like that – our lives had changed completely.

To squeeze a long story into one sentence: I found help. It wasn't exactly there the first night. Oh no.

Gib came home, discharged from the hospital without the correct equipment. The first morning he was home, he promptly fell, had to go *back to the E.R.* to take X-rays to make sure nothing had been dislodged (it hadn't).

Without the advice of my neighbor, Anna, I don't know what I would've done. She helped us obtain the medical equipment we needed from The Loan Closet, a wonderful place run by the non-profit Visiting Nurses Association.

Meanwhile, we were able to hire caregivers to look after Gib and myself.

Gib was going to make it. I had the first good night's sleep in weeks.

At last, I felt I could pull back and see if my new lifestyle was going to work. A big worry was getting the insurance company to pay. As Gib began to recover, he was able to take over the business of dealing with the long-term health care folks. Eventually, we were each able to each file claims to pay for the caregivers we needed around the house.

A New Book

The situation at home overshadowed the joy I felt at my new book's publication. Of course, there was no sustained publicity for the book, nor could I have had a book signing event even if I'd wanted to. Covid had seen to that. No group gatherings allowed.

But word of mouth is the best advertisement. I was amazed as, slowly, the comments came in. People were kind to write nice e-mails, and they warmed my heart. The messages gave me hope that indeed I had been able to reach others through my words in *Story of A Santa Barbara Birder.* (2020)

The most rewarding part of writing comes when individual readers tell you what the book makes them feel. Many readers wrote that they'd had a similar childhood, or that they felt the same way about birds. But others, unfamiliar with the birding world, seemed delighted to be ushered into it, if only briefly.

The reward was all mine, because writing saved me. Writing and birding allowed me to get through the rough days.

When I could get out to nature several times a week, and sit to watch the birds at my pond in between, I held those times precious.

If you can find what you need during these times of stress and pain, worry and change, then hang tight to it. Don't let the "you" part of you ebb away just because you're old and you think you should be resting.

Fight hard to stick with a routine that has time for yourself and your own projects.

5.

Pandemic Birding, Santa Barbara And Beyond

We are in the soup, in the lockdown, the red zone, the eye of the storm.

Here at the end of 2020, the Covid-19 coronavirus has our country and our state in a death grip.

In nearby Los Angeles County, one of the wealthiest regions in the world, people lie in hospital hallways and frontline nurses are worked to the maximum. No family gatherings, no holiday parties, isolation, quarantine, everything to tip you over the edge. The line in the sand is blurred: what's normal and what's over the top? What's O.K., and what's out-of-bounds? Paroxysms of guilt and fear envelope me on the one hand, and on the other I say, hey, wait a minute. I've got tools for this.

Birding During Covid-19, the First Surge

This chapter was written after what we remember as "the first surge" of Covid-19. Little did I know that the Omicron variant would once again bring our nation to its knees. At least by that time, we'd all had our vaccinations and boosters, not that it helped in some cases.

Regardless, the first surge was the most frightening, and initially, there was no cure.

My own lung disease made me more susceptible. I was cautious; the times when I went away from the house were birding trips.

Where could I go?

Empty parking lots were great. The car was accessible, and I was on level ground. Think of all the destinations that involved looking through the Tipuana tipu trees, those exotic street trees with small leaves and yellow flowers. They're often diseased by an insect, on which wintering birds like to feed.

In certain ways, Covid-19 has helped birding a lot. Fewer crowds of "non-birding" people, fewer cars. In addition, birders have more time and flexibility to get out since they're working remotely from home.

In truth, birding is itself a solitary pursuit. You may be with one or two persons, but you can be socially distanced from them while you're birding.

That's another reason this is a good Covid pastime: birders don't *talk*, they *listen*. They need to hear the chips and scolds of whatever birds are lurking in the bushes, hiding in the trees. Birders are like translators, taking the language of birds and turning it into meaningful identities, such as the Black Phoebe that's calling from the top of the roof, or the Bewick's Wren that just scolded from the myoporum hedge by the driveway. You may not be able to see these birds, but you can hear them and mark them on your list.

The reasoning here is that with my disease, talking is tiring. I talk on the "exhale." So every time I speak, I'm postponing that oxygen intake that's so desperately needed. But who wouldn't rather talk? Me for one. So I force myself to be quiet, and my birding is more productive.

Fall Birding 2020

I participated on a reduced level, when it came to chasing rare vagrants in migration. During fall migration, due to the complicated routes birds follow in order to leave snowy climates for subtropical areas, a bird's chances of getting lost go way up. That's when the birding gets exciting for those of us looking for new species that've never visited our county before.

Many species navigate their journeys south using landmarks, and if those guidelines are obscured by fog or rain, birds become disoriented. They may land along the coast, or wander far away from their desired route. Often these vagrants are lost at sea. All of us have heard of land birds hitching a ride on a boat occasionally. There's nothing cute or funny about this. The poor bird is completely exhausted, usually starving, and its last recourse is to land on a boat full of people. But there it is. And the people on board have no clue that the bird should be a thousand miles from there at its winter home.

We have a group of talented birders in this community. All are different, pursue separate lives, and each has something to contribute when it comes to bird finding. This fall the top awards go to our two Brit birders, Nick and Hugh.

Nick is a no-holds-barred laconic whirlwind. You won't get Nick to give you an explanation with even one extra word in it, but when it comes to bird finding, he goes way more than the extra mile. Marching up and down creek beds, driving to North County, and exploring every destination from Carpinteria to Cuyama, Nick does it all.

Hugh, on the other hand, is Mr. Birding-My-Neighborhood while on a bike, and we know how hard that is. Hugh can recognize the chip of a warbler, while he's pedaling away like mad. He's a primary school teacher, and a renowned one at that. But he finds the goodies, the rarities, and then we all go flocking to see what he's found.

Nick was responsible for introducing some of us to an industrial park in Goleta which was planted with Tipuana tipu trees. This fall, these trees were dripping with warblers, some of them rare and out-of-range. Early every morning, Nick posted news of the birds he'd found at this location, and the rest of us would show up later in the day.

I was thrilled to have an easy destination where I could bring my oxygen and hang out while watching some of these neat birds on their way through Santa Barbara to points south.

The 400 Club

There's a name for those of us who've seen more than 400 birds in our lifetime in Santa Barbara County. They call it "The 400 Club," which sounds like something a successful businessman would be in, not a bunch of birders. So I'll happily take my place, having a total of 455 birds in the county. And who has the *most* birds ever seen in the county? The tie goes to Paul Lehman and Brad Schram, both of whom have 463 birds! They ought to. They're the ones who turned us all on to birding the modern way, the exciting way, the way that keeps luring you out into the field just because *you* might be the one finding the next new bird for Santa Barbara County.

And the total of birds that've ever visited our county is 503 at this writing.

Meanwhile, back in real life, the fall stretched on. From excitement of a few good rarities (and they were snazzy!) the collective birding community sank in to boredom, suffering from Covid fatigue. Everyone was hungry for human contact, but fearful of the pandemic. Masks and social distancing were the absolute rule.

Dependent upon the kindness of my friends to chauffeur me around, I soon ran into difficulties. What if one of my friends got sick or couldn't take me birding? Was I to give up my lifeline during this crucial Covid lockdown?

Handicapped Birding With A Helper

The answer lay in my excellent group of caregivers. My new friend, was the organizer of some helpers in the Carpinteria area. These young women were amenable to coming to my house on a set schedule every month, to help me with all the challenges of living a life attached to a tube of oxygen.

You can imagine how grateful I was: somebody to monitor the oxygen tanks, somebody to help with every part of my life: cooking meals, dressing, bathing, and – why not? Birding.

They agreed to come out with me, handling the oxygen tanks with aplomb, giving me my special medicine (more on that later) in the field if necessary, loading my walker in and out of the car, and everything that goes with a birding excursion.

Here I describe the first time I ever took a caregiver out with me. I have given my caregivers the name "Jean" so as to protect their privacy.

Nature Journal: December 18, 2020
Lower Orpet Park

We get out of the car at one of the loveliest parks in Santa Barbara. This green space is named after E. O. Orpet, a park superintendent in the 1920s. Orpet, an accomplished English horticulturalist, was lured here when he saw how plants from around the world were able to grow in this climate.

I struggle out of the car, Jean lugs my oxygen from the backseat, and sets it up. What luxury.

I am vigilant for sparrows today. I glance down the sidewalk and see a group of little birds feeding in the dirt about 30 feet away. One by one, each bird ventures out of the tangle of plumbago and into the feeding group. Soon there are more than a dozen of them poking at the detritus under the oak tree there.

I whisper to Jean to grab my spotting scope. She gets it from the car and sets it up. I am thrilled to examine these White-crowned Sparrows now that I can see them through the scope.

Every time the flock gets scared, the birds scoot to the shelter of the bushes, then emerge again, one by one to feed on the ground.

*We see Fox Sparrows, Dark-eyed Juncos, and
California Towhees, all brownish and rather dull.*

*Jean doesn't believe me when I point out to her that
these birds are all different species. She assumes
they're all the same.*

*So here we are, me entirely transported to another
existence, away from my shrinking lungs and
wheezing chest, away from the doom and gloom
of the Coronavirus.*

*Soon, I turn and focus on the sparrow flock again, the
original one down the sidewalk, but this time it has a
new member. A White-throated Sparrow, not exactly
rare but not a common bird, sits primly on the edge
of the group, it's lovely white throat like a beacon to
those of us who can spot it.*

*"Jean! Look at the bird on the far left of the group!"
And I tell her what to look for.*

*"Oh amazing!" she says, although perhaps it really
isn't but she's catching my excitement.*

*We turn away at last, me exhausted from the effort, my
oxygen tank running out. No worries. Jean will transfer
me over to another tank.*

*She bundles me into the car, hooks me up to the other
tank, and gets into the driver's seat.*

I'm good to go, and I have a new birding helper.

As we drive off to the east along Alameda Padre Serra, I pass the house where my Faust grandmother, Nin, lived for awhile. She'd wanted a place near my mother and me, since my Dad was overseas during

World War II. There's a famous photo (in our family) of me held in the arms of my grandfather Faust taken at this house.

Perhaps I was pushed in a pram around Orpet Park? I know I played there as a child.

Everywhere I go birding these days, the past surrounds me.

Pandemic Birding

There's a general feeling that Covid-19 and its restricted lifestyle are conducive to folks becoming interested in birdwatching.

I agree.

However, when people start discussing how they've begun to notice birds while they were stuck in the long lockdown of the Covid-19 pandemic, it's difficult not to act smug, like, "I *told* you so." And, "Oh, okay, *finally* you see what we've been talking about?!"

When a friend calls me or writes me that they've had a bird sighting, and they're excited and enthused, it's hard to stay cool. Of course they've forgotten what we birders have been talking about all these years. This is important stuff, these birds you're seeing, and yes, they're marvelous.

One thing's for sure: we want to welcome everyone to birding. That way, we spread the news about birds and nature and it gets beyond our own established groups.

Fact is, despite the horrors of the Covid-19 pandemic, it has given birding a boost.

All through 2020, and now into 2021, I've been delighted to read editorials and opinion pieces, both here and in Great Britain. These pieces of news have a theme: "Our family was at home in lockdown, and we looked out the window and saw a woodpecker, a bluebird, a dove, a hawk, a pigeon…in the tree right there."

Often, it was a chance to let the younger members of the lockdown crew shine.

Children are observant; they have the sharper eyes. They brought their bird observations to their parents, and then the parents got interested, too.

I like this. It's our moment to snatch the lead. Lets everybody open the doors and see what's going on outside. Most restaurants are partially closed, same with retail stores, what can families do?

Our golden chance, our time has come, and it's full speed ahead National Audubon and birding! I now read articles online, with good descriptions of birds seen and enjoyed by many. These are genuine, eye-opening moments when people stop and discover birds. Their enthusiasm touches me.

Chasing Birds on Social Media

In addition, in the world of social media, you can find a different approach to birding. Here, birding has leaders and followers and if you sign on, you might be directed to find that Snowy Owl that was in Central Park in NYC. Or Barry, the Barred Owl, who visited the park for nearly a year. Barry seemed almost "tame" in the way she let people observe her during the Covid lockdown.

Right away, something as simple as birding, when thrown out into the Twitter sphere, became part of the "next thing" to do during the pandemic. After all, it's birds, it involves a chase, and it fits the social distancing/masks protocol. Indeed, several folks have set themselves up to manage bird alerts that keep track of what's going on in the bird world, where the birds are being seen, and how to reach them. If you "follow" that person on social media, you'll be part of a new set of birders.

I have nothing against this. My mantra has always been we need more birders, no matter what. If we don't have birders, who's going to tell us if a bird is scarce, or if it's multiplying like crazy, or if it's dying from some industrial foul-up? If people aren't out there noticing what's happening in the birding world, we might as well give up right now. We always need more bird enthusiasts, naturalists. They're going to save our planet.

But, this isn't a view shared by all, as some of the old guard can tell you. For it's this social media approach that has the ornithologists and biologists up in arms. Do they want folks running around scaring birds with camera flashes? No, they do not. Do they want all these bird locations publicized? No they do not. Are they afraid that birders on Twitter are not the kind of folks they'd really want to associate with? Perhaps.

I'm making a point here, and overstating some issues, but it's important to bring up all sides of the new "pandemic birding" phenomenon.

We welcome all these new birders. Whether they bring with them some changes in birding as we know it, we'll soon see.

Birding has already undergone an upheaval of great proportions, which can only be assessed after the pandemic has waned. Cancellation of birding tours, festivals, and Christmas Bird Counts has been a terrible blow. But, if we've managed to add new birders to our ranks, our responsibility is to teach them. Locations of certain sensitive species (owls are the best example) should ordinarily be held back to protect the birds' safety. This applies especially to the nesting season.

More on Pandemic Birding

One example of the pandemic birding-world phenomenon was a Swedish tour ship. During the year 2020, when a cruise ship no longer regularly stopped by a small offshore island where tourists were allowed to view a seabird nesting colony, devastation occurred.

The White-tailed Sea Eagle, a fierce predator of all seabirds, had already made a comeback in the area, and the eagles in turn were poised and ready for this break in the routine. No sooner did the eagles realize there were no "tourist interruptions" on the nesting island, than they came swooping down, making regular raids on the Common Murres that nested on the exposed cliffs. Researchers recorded that eagle traffic around the island soared by 760 percent, with a 92 percent *decrease* in human visitors.

As a result, the murres were flushed from their nests every time an eagle swooped in. Video footage showed temporarily abandoned eggs predated by gulls and crows every time the murres fled from the eagles. Overall, the influx of eagles led to a 26 percent drop in murre breeding performance compared to the previous decade. That's not enough breeding to sustain a long-term colony of Common Murres at this site.

The next step will be to see if the murre population rebounds when the tourist ships resume.

I have firsthand experience with seabirds and tourist boats. In 2018, Gib and I were passengers on a small tour ship in Scotland. Since there was a dedicated group of birders onboard, the ship's itinerary included several seabird colonies located on islands off the Scottish coast. We were able to approach these islands and view the masses of seabirds that nest on the ledges and cliffs. In addition, several stops were made where we got into a zodiac (small rubberized craft) and were brought from the ship to the islands. After disembarking, we could then wander about in the long, wet grasses, taking care to stay at a safe distance from the breeding birds, but close enough to get great camera views. The Common Murres, Razorbills, and puffins had a chance to become accustomed to human presence.

Despite our proximity to their colonies, the birds didn't seem to mind us. During our stays, I noticed no advances by birds of prey. Moreover, human interest in monitoring these important breeding colonies around the North Sea has grown in recent years. And, in talking to the ship's crew, it appears that throughout the United Kingdom, emphasis has refocused on seabirds. Some seabird populations are shrinking for various reasons, including a lack of proper fish to feed their young, and disturbances like those of the sea eagles.

In this same vein, my view is that birds are habituating to humans as a defense against predators. Think of hummingbirds and their nests placed near a hiking trail. Think of the species of birds that are increasingly accepting man-made nest boxes: Barn Owls using nest boxes have had outstanding success in agricultural and vineyard operations. The owls' ability to curb rodent populations has endeared them to landowners. Western Screech-Owls can be lured to a nest box, too.

In addition, American Kestrels, Tree Swallows, and Western Bluebirds will accept nest boxes, like several other species.

In one study in Berkeley, California, Cooper's Hawks were found to have raised robust offspring in suburban backyards over several years of observation. Perhaps the proximity to humans provides a better territory for raising youngsters than areas away from humans "out in the wild." These hawks chose tall planted trees in people's backyards.

However, the biggest success story of all is the spread of the American Crow throughout towns and cities across the U.S. Crows used to be found in agricultural fields, where they were often shot and killed as pests.

But there's no way people can shoot a crow or any species, once the bird is flying in a suburban neighborhood. And the crows know this. American Crows have learned that life among humans beats anything out in the countryside. They roost in groves of trees in a park, feed at garbage cans and dumpsters, at the beach or on a playground, and generally lead a good life where nobody is likely to harm them. Crows, members of the Corvid family like jays and magpies, have a reputation for being smart. Why else would they embrace human habitats so thoroughly?

6.

Birding Then And Now

Change.

Why do we fight it?

It's going to happen, yet when it does, we're shocked, certain the new way has flaws, certain the new generation will soon see the errors of their ways. Surely the way *we* used to watch birds was the best way.

We took the most accurate notes, went on the most difficult field trips, and produced the most new information.

All of this is true and none of it is true.

The new birders I meet are every bit as excited about birding as I am, perhaps in a different way.

First off, books on field identification are fewer. Instead of referring to books, as we used to do, birders go online; this is where birders seek information. They want quick snippets about a bird's habits, its range, its appearance.

Are bird books out of style? Will we ever refer to field guides again? Who knows?

I'll never forget when I got my hands on a copy of Ralph Hoffman's *Birds of the Pacific States*, published in 1927. Hoffman was one of the first directors of the Museum of Natural History here, and he and William Leon Dawson, an early founder of that same museum, wrote a lot of good information about birds in a Western setting. Not something to be easily found when I started birding, since most bird books featured Eastern species.

But our methods of birding differed from those today. Nobody loves a rarity more than I do. For regular birding, however, my buddies and I would go out, covering a patch of countryside that we enjoyed, or hitting several habitats or a selection of areas, to see what was to be found.

So little was known that we birders felt a sense of adventure and exploration. Some of the early gurus, like Guy McCaskie and Rich Stallcup, were figuring out patterns of vagrancy in Eastern warblers that had become misoriented.

Granted, birding was less democratic. There was a small coterie of advanced birders, some in Southern California, some in Northern California, and they were held together by their own friendship phone tree. The thrill of getting the call from a birding buddy gave it the personal touch. And everyone knew everyone in this ivory tower of birding.

Contrast that with today's birder. Let me explain about eBird, the worldwide database which keeps track of any list you make when you are out birding. Yes, there's an eBird website, where you can go to find out scads of information about birds in your area. However, the potent tool is the birding app that you put on your phone.

eBird, sponsored by the Cornell Lab of Ornithology, is a way of recording all the birds you see on a field trip. The birds you're most likely to encounter are in a big list on your phone, and you simply tap which ones you're seeing and how many. When finished, submit and off it goes to be read by others who subscribe to eBird all over the planet.

In this way, the eBird folks have hooked into social media trends, and birding will never be the same, for better or for worse.

eBird appeals to a younger crowd, too. There doesn't appear to be much appreciation of birding history. If you didn't begin birding in a place that had a birding mentor who could trace the trail of history, what do you do? You're going to get on Facebook, Twitter, Instagram, YouTube, and see if you can't figure it out.

In a few busy places, everyone rushes out to look at the same birds: those that've been posted on the county's rare bird alert. In fact, new birders appear to be rather blasé about these rare finds, because they aren't going out on their own looking for them.

Now, to the single greatest advance in birding *gear* in recent years: *optics.*

The newest binoculars and spotting scopes are fabulously clear, and accurate. Improved digiscoping has resulted in birders taking photos using the spotting scope as a magnifier. Even those photos using a cellphone, with the scope, can be useful as identification qualifiers.

Along with this goes the leap in the quality of hand-held cameras. The digital camera has revolutionized bird photography. Today, many more birders carry cameras. They know the value of an accurate photo when it comes to identification. However, multiply that by those folks who are not necessarily birders, but who are enjoying photographing wildlife. And they're increasingly pursuing birding, because they want to know the name of the bird they've captured on camera.

Whole tours are organized around not just looking at birds, but looking at them through a camera lens. These specialty tours often emphasize a group of birds, such as birds of prey, or tropical hummingbirds.

The participants on a photography trip proceed at a slower pace than those on a birding trip. Photographers need time and assistance in getting the best photos, whereas birders are in a hurry to find the next bird.

In addition, the recent pandemic may've hatched a whole other group of birders who, tired of being shut in and anxious to get out in nature, started to explore birding.

We cannot expect them to have the background that some of the rest of us have in birding, ornithology, natural history, and the like. In my view, it's imperative that we welcome anyone who wishes to explore the natural world and birds.

But there's one item that's the most significant of all: the *smart-phone.* Communication has always been paramount for birders, and now it's instantaneous. The time between the appearance of a bird and the message from the person who found it has shrunk from hours or days in the past, down to seconds or minutes today.

Widespread use of eBird for taking notes in the field has swept birding further into the realm of social media. Travelling birders need only possess a smartphone to hook up with eBird. They can then mark from a general list, the number and species of birds they saw on a particular outing at a designated location.

In this regard, various apps have taken the place of books and other materials. It's all there on a smartphone, and the new generation of birders won't spend time researching range maps, song samples, or photos, if they can find it online. *And* on their smartphone.

Interestingly, the rise in the use of social media has worked both ways for birders. It's gotten the word out right away whenever a hot new bird drops in to visit. However, with sensitive species, this is not a good way to go. Some sightings may need to be hidden to protect the birds from harm.

One complaint of those who're accustomed to the birding ways of old is that novices make mistakes, which then get entered into eBird, and may go uncorrected.

And yes a few errors elude the filters. However, in Santa Barbara County alone we have four or five excellent birders who regularly check eBird entries to monitor what goes through. They do a fine job.

More worrisome is the lack of good field notes. Birders rely on eBird, a quick way to enter a list of species seen in an area. But what about describing the bird you saw? Is a photo enough? I've heard stories of birders attaching photos of a bird, and it's *not* a photo of the bird they claim to have seen.

I believe my own notes have been reduced to perfunctory eBird lists. If it's an important finding or a special day, I compose a separate piece on my computer. No more hand-written notebooks, alas. My writing is too slow now to keep up with my notes, and the computer is a forgiving template. In the field, notebooks should still be used, but if there's Wi-Fi, they won't be.

Birding classes locally are full of students, and the bird tour companies have begun to sign up participants again. They're coming off a hideous dry spell due to two years of Covid cancellations.

For example, just from teaching birdwatching classes years ago, I have an idea of how two former students have been spending their time.

One, a local doctor, has traveled to all the nooks and crannies of the world looking for birds. He has a list of around 4,000 birds and he's only in the midst of his journey.

He graciously reminded me of another bird class participant of mine. This gentleman, a geologist, has seen 8,000 birds in his world wanderings. Now, that's a bunch. There are generally considered to be close to 10,000 species of birds on this earth.

My point is, I embrace anyone who shows an interest in looking at birds. We must welcome novices, old or young.

Indeed, members of the younger generations are the ones who've been the most active in saving the planet in other ways. These younger birders often arrive at birding because they've signed up to donate their time to a conservation cause. University campuses are one of the best places to find future birders. More than anything, an enthusiastic leader can be the catalyst.

However they reach you, if you have a chance to mentor a new birder, please do so. The future of our wildlife depends upon it.

The Last Word

When I asked a mentor about the difference between birding then and now, he said, "Alas, now *fewer* birds and *fewer* places to observe them, due to habitat gone or access denied."

Now that everybody's noticing birds, we're going to have to get much more serious about restoring bird habitats. Global warming is the culprit. I know we can save the birds, but we have to try much, much harder.

7.

The Covid Journals

I wasn't prepared for the Monday whammy, which turned into the Tuesday tumble, which became woeful Wednesday. I wasn't feeling my normal self.

I had no energy, and my pulse oximeter was not happy with my blood oxygen levels. This means that oxygen isn't getting through from my lungs to my blood. It's the result of lung scarring from the mysterious virus that attacked me.

I had it all figured out, until I didn't. And things began to go south, as they say.

I called my pulmonologist, a patient man. He had suggestions about some medications to try. Then, I ordered a new, higher-volume oxygen concentrator for my home.

But of course it's the mind that takes over and runs you up and down and back and forth. You want to scream. But stop. I want to be out in nature.

So this afternoon, I walk out onto the deck with a view of the garden. My pond is there, with water trickling into one end of it. The shrubs in the drought-tolerant landscape are thirsty due to the continuing drought, but they're gray and restful. It's a beautiful evening, warm and quiet.

I bring out my camera and my binoculars and set them on the table, for the hundredth time.

Then my heart pounds to a halt. I reach silently for the camera, click it on, hold my breath, and take a few bursts of photos of the bird that's calmly bathing there.

It's a *Yellow-breasted Chat.*

A Yellow-breasted Chat is a true skulker. They're hard to see, even on the breeding grounds. The males growl, chatter, whistle, and generally carry on like noisy jokers. They're easy to locate by sound, but you seldom get your binoculars on one. Although difficult to survey, local populations of chats in the West appear to be doing fine.

However, in winter, chats are rare and unusual. And they are completely silent. They all head south mostly to Central America, where the insects they hunt are plentiful. Winter records of chats are very few in California. And this would only be the fourth bird ever to spend the winter in our county.

Right here is my medicine. Quietly, unobtrusively, with no fanfare, no warning: an important contribution is in front of me. Nobody is telling me what to do or how to do it. But I know from years of study that this is how the scientific record gets built. Day after day, bird after bird, described with careful notes.

Nature always works for me, and birding is its pulse. These winter days I reach for my binoculars time after time. Even if I don't go anywhere, I have birds right in my garden. And that's my medicine cabinet, the one that has a cure for almost any ailment.

Yet my condition continued to deteriorate.

I thought I knew my body. Hadn't I watched this vessel bend and strain under the pressure of a lung virus? Didn't I learn quickly what the danger signs were of moving around with less oxygen than I needed?

The reason? I had the Covid-19 coronavirus for a week before I realized what was wrong with me. By the time I contacted my doctor, it was almost too late.

Breathlessness – worsening.

Tired feeling – worsening.

And so it went, on through those days of not feeling right, but not calling anyone's attention to it.

Boom! I got the call on January 14 from my doctor: Joan, you are positive for Covid-19, you need to go to the hospital now.

Whaaaaatttt ?

None of my caregivers nor my husband ever tested positive for Covid-19, but somehow, I had it. And I was terrified.

Nature Journal: January 14, 2021
Santa Barbara Cottage Hospital

On a winter day, highs in the 70s, blue sky above, I sit huddled in a wheelchair outside the section of ER that's designated for Covid patients. A nurse wheels me in and deposits me in a bed positioned lengthwise in a long, narrow room. It's a "midnight snack kitchen" for the Emergency Room staff, that's where I am.

Cabinets and a sink on one side of the room, and here I lie, waiting, for a long five hours. A few times a nurse and once a doctor come in, give me a poke, and say, "Boy, your lungs are noisy!"

They wheel me down a few halls for a CAT Scan. When the I.V. breaks off inside my arm, I scream like a wild cat. That hurts! "It's OK, we have the picture," says one of the nurses. They don't have time to mess around with people's comfort much. Can't blame them.

I am as breathless as ever, which is to say that's the new worseness that I've been feeling. I am falling asleep... they've started dripping some meds into me. I doze off.

Later the afternoon of the 14th: Ah... the time when you're alone in the hospital room and you can see there's an outside and a sky with dusk coming on.

It's very hot outside. Cool in here, oxygen whooshing up my nose at six liters per minute, I'll be OK on that.

For late lunch, I gulp down chicken noodle soup that came with a tray that appeared. You can't order, it's a set menu on the Covid floors. I had the soup and the salad. My phone is broken, so they don't know anyone's in my room and they never call and ask me for my food order, so I take the leftovers. I hoard the cookies, just in case I need them tonight.

For dinner, a piece of white cod sits alone in splendor, nestled up against an equally white bed of rice. A bright orange sauce has found its way over the top of the cod. Should I partake? Opt for the try-anything mode. Result: no good. Oh well.

I wonder if this hospital can fix me for the fourth or fifth time? I've had so many procedures, but I keep popping back.

Enough in the past. I like the way I look right now, with my pulse oximeter band across my forehead and my hair a mess, my hospital gown falling here and there due to all the cords and tubes coming out of me, plus the oxygen tube issuing from my nose. Ah, what a life I never thought I'd have.

You just can't imagine it, can you, all the stress and anxiety your body will have to withstand?

I walk over to the window; I'm on the ground floor and I have a lovely view. The earth outside, covered with lumpy landscape bark, shows green weeds beginning to push through. I can see the point where the earth meets the base of the plant, which is like seeing one of the two horizons. The other is the sky.

And when I see the sky and the earth, I am reassured that things are going to be stable. Immutable.

Why not try to do a bird list from my window?

Rising above the patio roof to the west, the street trees, pale sycamores with leafless branches, arch against a blue sky. I don't have my binocs with me, but I can see there are three Eurasian Collared-Doves slowly moving about in the tops of those sycamores. They have chunky gray bodies, and the light catches their square tails.

Twenty years ago, this bird was nowhere to be found on American shores. And then... somebody brought one and released it, and there you have the rapid spread of the little dove who's growling coo used to remind us of a French village. No more. The world is shrinking, and collared-doves are an example of globalization.

So I mark my eBird list with three doves, and four American Crows, which had flown by the window earlier, one actually carrying a stick in its talons. Nesting material is already part of the bird's instinct. It's been so warm.

And that's my first Cottage Hospital list for eBird! If I record whatever I see and register it, I'm adding to our knowledge of bird life.

Covid Incarceration

I'm trying to compare this hospital visit with others, and nothing comes close. There are four floors of Covid patients here now, and two ICUs devoted to the disease. The staff doesn't want to come into my room unless they have to, because full protective equipment is required. Nurses come in, and they're buried in masks and shields, paper garments, paper booties, paper hats. A wild party, but a sober one.

Nobody is having fun. The nurses are trying to stay positive, but every so often they slip and you can tell the toll this disease is taking.

The rooms are palatial, and cold. Only one bed to a room and nobody to talk to. The halls are like a morgue – no visitors anywhere, no banging doors, no laughing kids. Staff pared way down. Silence. It's too quiet.

I understand. I feel for the poor nurses. I try not to ask for extras. When people next door to me may be dying, I'm ashamed to disturb a nurse with my petty needs.

A special technician lady comes in to give my heart a sonogram test. She can't tell me the result, but she keeps saying, "I'm glad you came in," as if I'd just stopped by to quickly have a heart test, then be on my way. It sounded ominous, too. "I'm glad you came in."

At last, I get a break today, January 17. Dr. Litten rushes in. I like him. He grabs the pulse oximeter thing off the end of my finger, says "you don't need this!" and now I can write without having that pulse machine in my way.

Dr. Litten is casual. To all my questions about Covid, he replies "We just don't know." He's tired, of course, bone tired, weary of the whole situation.

The chief problem is that *everyone's different*, a roadblock to making generalizations about Covid. Twins react differently, siblings react differently, men and women react differently. No time yet for the long-term studies that medicine requires to bolster certainty. Risk is everywhere in these stages of the pandemic.

Coming Home

I come home on January 18, Martin Luther King, Jr. Day. I am full of myself, getting out of that hospital, having survived Covid, woo-wee look at me. What a warrior.

Being home is absolute heaven. My own husband, still strong, and my caregiver are always there for me. My oxygen supply machine steadily beats its rhythm of life.

However, the next day and the day after that, Covid has a parting joust at my body. An energy-sapping fatigue fills my days. I know I'm improving, but I can barely lift my arms and legs.

That and a tendency to vertigo are the worst of it.

Every day, I wake up to this tired feeling. No energy. It was bad when I had Covid, but now it's even worse.

Doc says six weeks is normal recovery time, if you have regular lungs.

I'm okay and on I go. It's just that I am needing to take some time here for recovery, and nobody told me!

One more recovery? Down and up, up and down, adjust, calibrate, backwards, forwards, the two-step of life. You better put your left foot forward if that's what's called for, not your right. You better have that mind of yours working to assess how your body is doing, too.

And then there's my heart. My heart that had to work so hard during Covid that it got tired. As in failure kind of tired. So it's not as strong as it was. As my cardiologist says "Joan, your heart is an innocent bystander, it's all the fault of your lungs!" The lungs can't get the oxygen they need quickly enough, which forces my heart to go into double time. And that's the nasty calling card that Covid has left with me.

8.

Slow Birding And Hospital Tours

A Hummer and a Vine

One day I was sitting on the deck in a chair about two feet away from the red trumpet vine that climbs over the pergola.

The vine is in bloom now with 4-inch long tubes of bright red that flare out at the tip. However, the nectar is located at the base of these beautiful flowers. No local bird has a bill long enough to reach deeply in order to gather the nectar.

As I sat there, a splendid male Allen's Hummingbird whirred up to the vine and perched on the first long blossom he could find. I watched as his tiny form, with the miniscule feet, held onto a part of the stem that ended in a red flower. Immediately, the hummer stuck his bill into a spot that *looked like it had been used before* and started sucking at the sweet juice. I could see that already on the outside of this flower, a pinprick hole had been punched. Into the hole the bill went, just like a straw into a bottle, and when the bird was finished, it moved on to the next flower, and then another, until he had checked most of the blooms on that side of the vine.

Afterwards, he darted over to the olive tree, where he commands a post overlooking the garden.

That orange-throated Allen's Hummingbird let me see how creative he could be with those huge flowers. He just went in the side at the base of the bloom and found the sweetness that he needed without going in from the top.

Moreover, when I saw the Allen's Hummingbird so close, without binoculars, I realized once more how inventive these tiny beings have to be to survive, despite our mild Santa Barbara climate. The nights can be cold, nectar is scarce, and the ability to go into torpor often saves the hummers from freezing.

But the vine-tapping occurred in the flash of a few seconds. I was knocked over! Did I dream it? No, it was one of those pieces of life in nature that I would have missed had I not been "sitting around watching."

Juncos That Do It All

Another day, I observed a male Dark-eyed Junco. He was a slick specimen with a shiny black head, a pink bill, and pale brown sides bordering a white vest. Since there wasn't much going on with migration, I thought I might as well study one of the locals to see if there was anything I could learn.

It being the spring mating season, this male junco is under pressure to attract a female. His feathers have to be in the best shape possible, to stay bright and healthy, thereby sending a message to a prospective mate that "this guy would be a good provider."

Anything that dulls the gloss of a male's appearance at this time is bad for his standing in the evolutionary race to pass on his genes. Researchers have long believed that females choose mates based on the spic-and-span appearance of the male, thereby signifying he'd be a healthy gene-bearer for her young.

However, males may have other tricks up their feathery wings. Recently, a study of a species of tanager revealed that the feathers of both females and males contained the same pigments, casting doubt on the theory that males may have more of the bright carotenoids (resulting in orange, red, and yellow color) in their systems.

Furthermore, one study found that ultimately the males' feathers were constructed in such a way as to reflect more light than a female's. So with a tiny lengthening or shortening, a broadening or narrowing, a twirling or a tweak, a male's feathers catch the light in lovely ways, possibly adding to the female's delight. Female feathers lack these add-ons.

Does that mean the older theory that bright colors are evidence of good health and the ability to forage widely is out? Not necessarily. But it could mean that some males are sharp-looking, and it has nothing to do with the fact that they're good providers.

All this went through my mind as I saw the Dark-eyed Junco hop into the pond, then spend minutes splashing around. An orderly sequence of feathers got wet. First, he dipped his head and bill in. Next came the outer feathers of the wing and tail, then he worked his way, shaking the water off, then dipping and scooping until his whole body was soaked. Each time, the feathers were lifted up and away from the skin, so it could get wet.

About fifteen minutes later I saw movement on the ground in between shrubs in the backyard. I have a thick layer of mulch covering the soil in the garden. And at first I thought I saw a gopher burrowing.

But no, it was the male Dark-eyed Junco.

He was on Round Number Two: the dust bath. Birds don't generally take a dust bath if there's plenty of water around, but in some cases they'll take both. The junco was submerging himself in a little scrape in the topsoil, and as he did so he flicked some dirt over one wing and then the other, then shook it off. He nestled down in that warm spot to take a sun bath.

I was glued to the sight of this elegant, common bird, one I see every day, and the pains he took to keep in good shape.

Either by a water or dust bath, birds need to keep their feathers clean of surplus oils and unwanted parasites. In the evolutionary race, the one where the females are mate-shopping, a male's shiny plumage, or lack of it, is item number one on the list of desirable characteristics.

Nesting Above the Washer/Dryer

All of a sudden, it's upon us. The Red-tailed Hawks are circling high, the crows are dive-bombing them if they can; the California

Thrasher sits at the top of the hedge singing his head off. His gurgling, chittering, and chattering are no match for the mockingbird, but the mocker sings down the street farther away.

The Bewick's Wrens have decided that yes, our messy back porch laundry room is okay with them one more year, making this the fourth year they've chosen to nest there.

And on my walks through Manning Park I've discovered a White-breasted Nuthatch nesting in the crevice of a manmade stone wall, a foundation of the old toolshed that's been there for ages. I've never seen a nuthatch that's not in a tree, but hey, it's a great sighting for the breeding bird survey.

And the way I look at it, the more we can get birds to breed, the more they will survive to increase the numbers of birds on earth. More nests. More habitat that encourages safe nesting.

Our Bewick's Wrens are inhabiting a homemade cardboard box that resembles a pointy, three-sided Swiss Chalet. Gib fit it under the eaves of the roof of our back porch. Now, five feet above the washer/dryer unit, six little mouths open wide every time the Mom and Pop come flying in. The adults hurry back and forth to feed those youngsters.

The adults' bills are thin, curved. They grasp mayflies, spiders, and bugs of all kinds. A parent flies in, stuffs a couple of gaping mouths full, then leaves immediately. Sometimes they aim to do clean-up on their way out. They pick up a fecal sac, the membrane enclosure that surrounds one of the nestling's poops; the adults pick the sac up and fly out with it in their bills. So fun to watch this. So efficient. Only helpless songbird babies use fecal sacs, but few humans are aware of them. Pretty cool.

Today we had a scare. A Scrub-Jay was hanging around the entrance to the nest.

We shooed him off, but he has the power to destroy the whole nest, along with the nestlings.

But by and large, our homemade nest was pretty good for the young Bewickers. We only have a few more days to go and I hope the other youngsters can make the break as successfully as the first one did.

The first one just hopped out the back, tumbled to the floor, then flew up to the top of the hedge, and was gone. These outlier youngsters will be fed by the parent birds if they're in the vicinity of the nest, so the idea is to let them go once they've fledged. Putting the birds back in the nest isn't necessary.

And it happened. We only lost one fledgling, the rest were off and gone in a moment. Now I hear them singing from our hedges and I wonder if it's one of "ours."

Life Now

I'd had my two and a half years.

But in early 2021, Covid-19, the Coronavirus, invaded my body. Miraculously, I survived a hospital stay and actually began to feel better.

As we now know, Covid can do long-term damage to a patient's internal organs. In my case, my heart, already straining to keep the oxygen going in and out of my lungs, was vulnerable. Covid left its mark. I was blessed to recover, but my life has changed.

Breathing capacity down, heart rate too high.

Your heart is "in the red zone," the cardiologist pronounces. My heart is straining under the pressure to produce the oxygen to fill my lungs. Mechanical difficulties.

Day in and day out, I have ways of getting the life-giving oxygen I need: one is a fixed stationary oxygen concentrator, which stays in the entryway of the house. Its reassuring hum and rhythm have been a background to my life since the day I returned home from the hospital over two years ago.

When I'm inside the house, I am always attached to a cannula (nose tube) that's hooked up to a 50-foot plastic tube that feeds the oxygen from the stationary machine mentioned above into my nose.

Like a strange urban cowgirl, my looped oxygen tubing comes with me, hands-free, as I go about my activities. Otherwise, the tubing is constantly getting caught on rugs or pieces of furniture. But it's a great feeling to be able to move about with two hands free. And the tubing even reaches as far as the deck outdoors.

When I leave the house now I require the big green "E" tanks, those cylinders that have to be filled by a special machine that's located in the garage. Gib and my caregivers see that these tanks are always kept full. Unlike the "concentrator," the green tanks don't take oxygen out of the air themselves; consequently they are purer, but when they're done they're out of oxygen. No way you can plug them in and use a battery to recharge, so that's a pain.

Other than the oxygen conveyors, life is SLOW. Quiet. The cardiologist's warning frightens me. I understand that my heart is tired. I don't blame it.

Exercise is a necessity and always on my mind. How can I use up this precious energy I was given to live with, so that I can sleep at night, rest and relax?

I need to exercise my lungs daily, push them gently to work for me, without harming them. I can do that on the treadmill. Twenty minutes per day very slowly, measuring constantly with my pulse oximeter. Safe and slow and controlled. That's the way we do it now.

Soon, I contemplate a new procedure, a double angiogram to see if I can qualify for one of the first drugs ever invented for my disease.

My doctor and a colleague have been studying the pressure that builds up in the heart when it has to pump oxygen to the blood through diseased lungs. This latest drug was certified by the FDA less than a month ago. It's administered in puffs from an inhaler and is able to give the lungs a boost for exercise and mobility. It would be such a boon to me. So we'll see if my heart is in a condition to be able to benefit from this new drug.

There are no cures for my disease, so this is the frontier of medicine and I'm contributing.

Notes From The Hospital: March 2, 2021
Angiograms And Other Adventures

At the moment I'm lying in the pre-op room for people who've been admitted to the hospital for a minor procedure. This isn't the full-on O.R. treatment, no. This is what they call a "procedure," which is probably a synonym for, "You could die, but since it's elective, there's no recourse."

I had two doctors who planned to prod and poke and measure me. This was okay, because the goal was worth it.

My pulmonologist has a bee in his bonnet about a new drug he and a colleague have been working on. Unbelievably, the drug was one designed for folks like me. If taken properly, the drug just might give me the extra energy I need to go birding and do more exercise even with my damaged lungs.

However, there are conditions. I would need to be examined by a cardiologist along with a pulmonologist, to measure the pressures in my heart and my lungs, making sure I'm a candidate for the new drug.

So I'm lying here, having been awake since 5 a.m. – fasting – and I could use a cup of coffee. I hear others getting the initial directions over in their cubicles, "gown opens in the back, everything off including your underwear" from each of the nurses. I've put my clothes in a bag, and begin to read my e-book.

8:30 a.m. comes and goes. Hurry up, folks!

Aha, here he is! A nice young man wheels my gurney off to wherever I'm supposed to go. And his name is Fred, or Dave, but we have a conversation. And it's always about Santa Barbara High, because so many of us locals have attended, and it's "once a Don always a Don!" Great note to begin and end on for a little journey through the hospital corridors, up and down in elevators and eventually, down, down to what feels like a basement as he pushes me along.

The double doors open automatically, and it's like we've arrived at a party. There's loud rock and roll music playing. Various male techie types (are they nurses?) are climbing around fixing apparatus, putting things where they belong, setting up. I'm immediately introduced to Harry or Larry, (who's significant other "loves birds, feeds birds, etc.") and we're off to chatting about that, while I'm then greeted by my pulmo doc and the cardio doc.

Is this a procedure or a party? I haven't been to a party in way too long. What with Covid and all. The feeling is: let's have fun!

They roll me onto the flat bed operating table where I'm supposed to lie, and I try to look around. I see a big open dark room that looks as though it can be used for anything the medical profession wants. A huge computer screen looms, various track lights shine here and there. Where is this place?

One guy is busy making up an I.V. to go into my left arm, where they can drip the stuff, "conscious sedation," into my body.

Elsewhere people are bustling around, but I never see the doctors. They're behind me, I guess, and then I realize they're putting a shield over my right side so they can access my neck for one of the tests. Made of fabric, this doesn't bother me. But I can't see a thing.

As the liquid infuses, I realize I'm half-asleep, but I can also hear what's going on. The docs work quickly. Pulmo first. No issues. He's in and out pretty quick, although I think they had to enter through my groin, not my neck.

Then comes cardio doc and I hear something about "blockages." What??? They're telling me there are two blockages! When he suggests coming back for another operation to put a stent in I say no, fix it now!" I remember that clearly.

And I guess he did.

Two angioplasties, both where they found some narrowing of the heart and of a vein, and he inserts the little widening balloons and leaves them there. A huge advance in cardiac medicine, these stents are now common.

I'm not sure where all this damage comes from, but Covid is responsible for the dirty work on my heart.

Okay then, it's over and the only worry now is I have to stop bleeding. The drugs they give you to thin your blood must be induced to stop the bleeding with another set of drugs. Poor ole body.

I'm rustled up to I.C.U., where patients recover from surgeries. Of course, I remember it all too well: the blasted "owl" notes emanating from the computer screen high above my bed. How they drove me crazy the last time I was here. Now I accept this as part of the hospital routine.

"Boop, boop, boop, boop" goes the Flammulated Owl line (that's the oxygen line).

"Bip-bip-bip-bip" goes the Northern Saw-whet Owl (blood pressure line).

STOP. The last time I was in here I thought I'd never

get out! And I've had two years of wandering this land, attached to a life-giving oxygen cannula of course, but two years! I am so lucky.

The nurse yells at me to quit moving my thigh, I must remain flat. This is all to prevent bleeding, but it seems a bit out of proportion. I am once again ensconced in my book.

Food comes in, but since I'm not permitted to move my right hand due to a wound area there, I cannot partake. I'm starving, but what do you do? Eating with my left hand is a messed up effort and I spill chicken noodle soup down the front of me. Fun. I'll wait till dinner.

And so the hours roll by, and the night comes quickly down. It's all familiar. The lonely dinner hour, the nurses rushing around. Me staring at the cellphone for company and reassurance.

Surely this is my last rodeo at lovely Cottage Hospital. Great place, but do you really want to get to know every floor?

The best part comes at 9:30 p.m., when the nurse gives me meds and leaves. Then I hope that every little somnambulant granule will step up to the plate and work their wonders.

And they do. I sleep all night long. Guess I really was knocked out.

The next day is delightful. The day of going home. I'm filled with anticipation. Three wonderful doctors come to see if I'm doing alright: my pulmo, my cardio, and my general practitioner – truly committed these men are. Two are from India, one is from South Africa.

I'm in my wheelchair, ready to go.

I've seen all the levels of Cottage Hospital now; I've had the grand tour.

The party in the basement was interesting, and I've got new body hardware inside myself to show for it. But I think I'll skip the next time I'm offered a visit at Cottage.

PART III:
Onward And Outward

9.

Rescued

The Ides of March was good to me. My new medicine arrived and I started taking it that day, March 15, 2021.

I'm not sure how much longer I could've survived breathing at the level of oxygen that remained. My body grew weaker and weaker. All I could do was sit. Every movement plunged the pulse-oximeter lower and lower and my heart rate was jumping higher.

Weaker and weaker I grew, unable to do the treadmill. I was eager for the new medicine. But that first weekend, after I read about the new medicine, I was sure I couldn't do it, and *afraid of trying and failing*.

The medicine sounded complicated when I read about it. As usual, I dismissed the whole concept, was sure it wouldn't work, and swore to discontinue use after two weeks if I saw no improvement.

I begged the nurse to come to me sooner rather than later. Finally, that Monday, she knocked at the door. The nurse had a perky manner. Everything she said or did was recorded on her iPad. She lived in Grover Beach, and I was one of her patients far away.

She's hired by specialty pharmacies, similar to the one that sent me my medicine from Pennsylvania, to oversee patients like me. She undid the special inhaler, and showed us how to put it together again. It was made up of over a dozen little plastic parts. I was sure I could never manage to fit all of them back together.

Fear, fear, fear. When will I ever learn that I always fear the wrong things?

I know I can't do this, it's never going to work.

But I'd underestimated my husband, that clever man. He took it on immediately, figured out how to put the contraption back together once it was undone, then taught the caregivers how. Gib did it all.

From then on, he was the one reminding me to "take my meds." That needs to be done on a tight four-hour schedule during the day. Just how much leeway I can get remains to be seen. I'm experimenting.

Immediately, I noticed improvement in my breathing even after a few days. Gradual, oh so small, but definitely there.

Also, there were side effects. I'll skip the details, but the side effects are not fun. You play, you pay.

There are times when my numbers do not plunge as low as I expect, even when I'm breathless. There are times when I'm on the treadmill and the pulse-oximeter is reading well into the 90s before I do a session of walking.

There are times in the morning, after my treatment, when I can get up and brush my teeth and do my flossing, whereas I used to be unable to do that. My body is getting stronger, I may be gaining weight, and may be getting more muscle strength since I am trying to lift weights a little bit. My voice is stronger and I am not coughing any more.

I also gasp for breath a little less.

But there's nothing that compares with the feeling of your body going *uphill* and improving rather than *downhill* and growing desperate. And that makes up for everything else.

Going Forward

I'm trying to adjust my psyche to a new way of living. I am afraid to be too hopeful, but I want people to know I'm feeling better.

In the end, is it all a matter of confidence?

I am strong. I am strong. I need to tell myself that a million times a day.

Give me the confidence in my body's ability to perform.

If I can be calm, I can perform. If I waste energy on anxiety and worry, I am exhausted. My physical condition has got to come first.

Just had the thrill of my life, when my pulse-oximeter (which measures oxygen in my blood) didn't plunge below 77 after a bathroom break, but stayed at 77 then went right back up to 81 and lingered there.

Nobody knows the freedom these numbers give me: my life is structured on a grid from 50 (disastrous) to 90 plus (wonderful, normal). If I get way down into the 50s and 60s, I reach for my mask, with the oxygen flowing out of it in a central tube. The mask can usually get my oxygen up faster.

And so it goes, the details, the little things. The building blocks of life.

I feel as though I'm walking on the crest of a roof. If I fall one way, I'll be back with the invalids who can't participate in a normal life. If I fall in the other direction, I'll be with the "back to life" crew.

Truth is somewhere in between.

Anatomy of a Miracle Drug

I wish I knew the inside of my body better so I could see what's happening in there. The nebulizer medication that's pulling me back to life appears to be opening up the tiniest blood vessels in my lungs so they can carry oxygen better.

Little by little, I notice I can go to the bathroom without help, walk short distances by myself, lean over and pick something up off the floor.

Weird naps overtake me so that I just doze more in the day than at night.

So it is *now*, and there's no future.

It's coffee in the morning, a look at the news on my phone, a try at the "spelling bee" in the *New York Times*, a try at WORDLE, texting with my daughter Jen, hearing about the grandkids, getting ready for the first "treatment" of the day.

And I can read or write whenever or whatever I want all day. I can watch birds, walk with my walker, and all this time I'm using my pulse-oximeter to see the heartbeat numbers as well as the oxygen levels. My heart is what needs my help more than anything.

I've added hope, but I have no idea where it's going, do I? Out of my hands. Destiny is pulling me along, whether I want it or not. And yet, I still think I have some control... silly... just sit back and take the ride... that's what you've always done.

What I Learned About Viruses Before Covid Ever Appeared

I want to return to a pre-lung disease time in my life, a time when I was not sick. What I learned has meaning for my life now.

One day in 2016, I was perusing the program from the UCSB Arts and Lectures series. Here in Santa Barbara, this organization brings the best speakers on a variety of topics to the university. I have a friend who's interested in science, and we usually go together.

The subject for this lecture was complicated, having to do with genes, viruses, and how they interact. Therefore, a preparation mini-lecture at the Santa Barbara Public Library was held a day beforehand. The main lecture was to be given at UCSB by Jennifer Doudna, the well-known microbiologist from UC Berkeley.

That's why I found myself at the Public Library, signing the attendance sheet and hurrying up to the front row where my friend had saved a seat. It felt like high school but a thousand times better. The room was packed.

Up to then, I'd never heard of CRISPR and gene editing. But I sensed this was important stuff, and I wanted to try to learn more. The topic had to do with the revolutionary gene-editing tool that Professor Doudna and others have been working on for several years.

Without getting too far in, let's say that CRISPR is a tool that geneticists can use to fight viruses in the way that bacteria do, among other things. In their DNA, bacteria develop clustered repeated sequences, which can remember and destroy viruses that attack them. That's how immune systems adapt to fight each new wave of viruses.

We also learned about RNA, the molecule that Doudna studied, and that later was used in one of the vaccines against Covid-19. (At that time we knew nothing about Covid-19.)

I was mesmerized after Professor Doudna's talk, and I could see how complicated her work was.

Eventually, I grasped the importance of microbiology and the revolution in medicine that was taking place before my eyes. However, it was not until the Covid-19 pandemic that I understood how science could come forward and create applications for commercial companies to use in medicine.

Of course, this is what has happened in my own case with the pulmonary arterial hypertension. Early experiments had been carried out years before, and the medication was now targeted for a patient's use. That's how I got my nifty inhaler, which carries medicine straight to my lungs through the blood vessels, thereby supplying them with beneficial oxygen.

In my opinion, we're in an era comparable to that of the personal computer in the 1970s and '80s. This time it's microbiology and an examination of life itself. Currently, scientists are making discoveries based on close, painstaking studies of nature. They're looking at RNA, a special part of DNA that makes proteins, acts as a guide for enzymes, and can replicate itself. RNA carries genetic instructions from DNA in a cell's nucleus to the manufacturing region of the cell.

Back in March 2020, when the Covid-19 pandemic shut down the U.S., Doudna and her colleagues had been brainstorming amongst themselves. This was a time few had prepared for, when we needed to use cutting-edge experiments in microbiology to aid in the development of a vaccine. Scientists around the world came forward to help.

The lightning speed with which a successful vaccine was put forth will go down in history. Both Moderna, based in Cambridge,

Massachusetts, and the German company BioNTech, which partnered with an American company, Pfizer, began clinical trials.

By November 2020, when the results were in, "It was a bad day for viruses," Moderna leaders were quoted as saying in the book, *The Code Breaker*, by Walter Isaacson.

If you want an exciting story of science and nature and how it all eventually culminated in the successful production of vaccines, it's in this well-written account.

Isaacson closes with this quote:

> *"The invention of easily reprogrammable RNA vaccines was a lightning-fast triumph of human ingenuity, but it was based on decades of curiosity-driven research into one of the most fundamental aspects of life on planet earth: how genes encoded by DNA are transcribed into snippets of RNA that tell cells what proteins to assemble."* (Isaacson, page 447)

That paragraph stuck in my mind. I couldn't get it out. The idea was that all of the new science they'd discovered about viruses was simply another part of nature. Viruses and bacteria had interacted like this for billions of years. Scientists had been examining these workings over and over and they'd come to ground-breaking conclusions.

The conclusions are observations about nature and how it operates, and how we as humans have the knowledge to tinker with the workings of our own bodies. Our own cells and enzymes are the players here, and they've been going for centuries. No wonder they've perfected the environmental game of survival. We can borrow some of these tricks, but they are not new, they are just now being brought to light.

I am grateful for the top scientists from all over the world who contributed to breaking this "code" for tapping into ways to fight against diseases like the Covid-19 pandemic. We need to stay as informed as we can about the latest scientific discoveries.

References: *The Code Breaker: Jennifer Doudna, Gene Editing, and the Future of the Human Race*, by Walter Isaacson. Simon & Schuster, New York, 2021.

10.

Back To The Fun Of It

By the time June 2021 rolled around, I was ready to try birding. It had been such a long time since I'd been out in the field. My new medicine stirred my courage and made me want to try.

Up to now I hadn't the strength to sustain even 10 minutes of birding beyond the backyard. Could I really do it? Could I manage all of the oxygen tanks and still concentrate on the natural world around me?

No. Not without having a caregiver along to monitor the oxygen intake and to bring the proper tanks, my walker, the scope, and all that it took for me to get outside.

I'll never forget the first time I ventured out. I was anxious to see the female Snowy Plover, a tiny shorebird, that had chosen to nest on the wide open beach at Carpinteria. The last time a nest was successful here was in the 1960s, so this I had to see.

Below is the journal entry from my first day out birding after all my Covid-related health issues:

Nature Journal: June 7, 2021
Carpinteria State Beach

We pull up to the kiosk at Carpinteria State Beach Campground to get our day pass.

"We're here to see the nesting Snowy Plover," I say

brightly, hoping the ranger will say "OK, why don't you just go on (in without a fee)?" Well, he doesn't.

When we try to explain where the bird is located and ask about a parking place, he says construction has taken up all their handicapped parking spaces. What? I can't possibly walk as far as he's describing.

But we drive on in, cross the bridge over Carpinteria Creek. How many times have I hiked down along the creek and approached from the other side? Gives me a shiver at how quickly life can flip you over.

We spot the picnic table out on the sand that we're told is the marker beyond which the nest lies. Oh boy. We're at the right location.

No parking spot anywhere.

Kids in strollers, dogs on leashes, fathers dumping garbage, construction workers, everybody's busy.

Good, they won't notice us double-parked in a red zone.

Jean runs out to the beach to scout the area, meanwhile I'm in the front seat taking my treatment that's due at 11 a.m. I grab the magic inhaler, listen to the timer as I measure each puff, then rinse my mouth out and pour the contents of the cup out the car door. Easy as pie.

"It's right there behind that little hill!" Jean gasps as she returns.

I walk along beside Jean and the tank. We stop at a high spot, and I use my binocs to scan the beach before we take off. And there it is: the 2-foot-high wire exclosure erected by park staff to protect the Snowy

Plover. Inside, the female plover is huddled close to the dry sand, where she's incubating three eggs.

But in order to get even close enough for a blurry photo, I must cross a short distance of soft sand.

I take one look at the route, decide I have to try it, and off I go.

My feet aren't very responsive. In hiking boots I make them work. Clomp, clomp, clomp over the sand. They feel like swollen sponges, but they're doing their job. Closer and closer and finally near enough for a distant photo. That tiny shorebird.

At least the camera has a blurry memory of my first birding outing on oxygen.

Soon, I turn around and head back, Jean attached to me, and both of us yelling in delight. We don't care how silly we look, we've done it.

On this dark, overcast day, I have resumed birding. Sure, the outings are vastly different from the good old days, but if I can just get out there, I've got the key to all sorts of renewal. My confidence is up and I'm riding high all the way home.

After the excitement was over, I sat down to study the information about Snowy Plovers and this particular pair.

This female has a band on her leg, indicating she was hatched at Vandenburg Air Force Base in 2013. And that means this bird has been alive for eight years, a long time for a small, threatened shorebird.

Later, we learned that all three Snowy Plover chicks at Carpinteria were hatched and doing well. They were accompanied by their dad, the male plover, because the female had departed. Typical of this species, she may choose to attempt another nesting with a different mate, or just pack it in for the season.

Meanwhile, the male stays with the young, teaching them to forage for morsels in the mud, and to run back to the wire exclosure for safety. I'm so grateful to the parks staff and other volunteers who watched over the plovers from a distance, and explained to passersby what a special event this nesting was.

More Plovers

In 2022, up to three nests were active on Carpinteria Beach at this same location. I was able to see Nest Number 2 this year in its wire exclosure. We may be lucky to witness the start of another colony of nesting Snowy Plovers, just as they have at Sands Beach near UCSB. However, subsequent news tells of predation by a pair of Red-tailed Hawks in the area. The fledged plovers are defenseless, and can be easily picked off by a crow or hawk. This is what's so difficult about restarting a colony of plovers. At UCSB, many of the youngsters have to be taken in and raised by hand until they grow bigger.

"Fall" Shorebird Migration in Summer

For myself, I used to think summer birding in Santa Barbara was boring. By that I mean most of the nesting birds have had their young, and may have departed to higher elevations where there's more available food. I wanted to be in the high mountains when summer rolled around.

But when I learned that summertime can mean watching for shorebirds here at home, the scene got a lot more interesting. The shorebirds that come through in early summer are those that nest at northern sites – Canada and Alaska – and are on their way south already, by the end of June through July and August. Indeed, fall-shorebird migration takes place throughout the summer.

Furthermore, waterbirds such as herons and egrets arrive in

summer to Santa Barbara's beaches and estuaries. In a phenomenon known as post-breeding dispersal, we get to see a few species of birds that nest south of the Mexican border, and wander up here. The birds are almost always juveniles, because they're looking for new territories.

One of my favorite birding locations is Goleta Beach Park. In my condition, easy access is crucial. I drive with my caregiver to the far eastern end of the paved parking lot. There, we set up my walker, the oxygen tanks, and the spotting scope.

Behind me the narrow beach stretches towards Hope Ranch, and in front of me lies the big lagoon of Goleta Slough that drains into the sea. Birds are all around, roosting or feeding on the sandy banks of the watery channel. High in the eucalyptus trees on the bank opposite, I can't miss the rookery of Double-crested Cormorants, with their dark, thin necks reaching up from stick platforms.

It's a busy place.

Nature Journal: July 25, 2021
Goleta Beach

I'm pinching myself. This can't be real. It's too wonderful, too much fun... Weren't these days over for me months ago? Aren't I an invalid?

Apparently not.

Here I am on Goleta Beach on a Sunday morning, caregiver Jean manning the oxygen tanks, the walker, and the scope.

I'm looking for the Reddish Egret, a gorgeous, exotic egret with a purplish hue. I've seen several of these in my lifetime, but I want to see this one now.

My friend, Libby Patten, drives up. Together we take our scopes and look into the distance out past the slough outlet. And we locate a heron-shaped bird with

*long legs marching around in the wave's surge. That's
our bird! The Reddish Egret is strutting opposite a surf
fisherman, who doesn't even notice he's got an egret
at his elbow.*

*Other birders arrive. Libby and I are squinting through
our scopes at the Reddish Egret far away. What a
beautiful bird, tall, elegant, with long legs.*

Next day*:*

*This morning finds me back at Goleta Beach peering
into the fog.*

*A Great Egret, a Snowy Egret, and yes, there's the
Reddish Egret – wading in the lagoon. Fog swirls
are catching the light off the incoming tide, making
pale gray reflections in the water. A ray of sun
peeks through.*

The tide slides in, the Reddish Egret shuffles along.

*Suddenly the egret prances forward with wings wide,
quickly moving to one side or the other. Then abruptly
it ducks and covers its head with broad wings, making
an umbrella. Moving along, this unlikely umbrella of
wings creates shadows on the surface, which attract
fish. At last, the Reddish Egret spears a fish. One quick
flip, swallow, and the fish is gone.*

*As the Reddish Egret continues its fairy dance in the
lagoon, the fog comes in and out. Gentle ripples of
gray surround the pale purple bird. When its wings
are lifted, I see deep pink on the flanks and sides.
Against the background of cold seawater, the egret's
movements are a mysterious dance.*

*These egrets are rare this far north, for they prefer
the warm bays of Mexico and Baja. This one has*

*travelled far, but, like so many other young birds, it got
squeezed out of its natal territory by the adults. And
off it goes… wandering up the coast from one beach
to another. A risky time for young birds to be learning
the ropes, but that's how they do it.*

*I could watch a Reddish Egret all day, doing its water
dance in the lagoon. As familiar as Goleta Beach is to
me, my eyes are opened again. Despite the parking lot
and busy people, the rhythm of nature continues. The
Reddish Egret hunts, the fish swim in from the sea, the
tide ebbs: is anybody watching?*

Birders are. I am.

In most of the older field guides describing Santa Barbara's bird life, the authors talk about "El Estero." Early birders and other observers complained about this low basin and its ripe smell on hot days when the water level was low. However, they marveled at the way the place attracted shorebirds. Many descriptions of shorebirds by William Leon Dawson in his famous *Birds of California* were written about birds he observed at El Estero around 1920 or so.

I decided to find out exactly where El Estero was, and you know what?

It's not absolutely clear, but it certainly was more than just what's known as the Bird Refuge.

El Estero was a low point stretching up from the beach, under the railroad tracks through lower Santa Barbara, south of Montecito Street. It was bordered by Santa Barbara Street on the west and Salinas Street on the east. A big chunk of caked dry flatland for some of the year, El Estero would flood in winter rains and high tides. However, during the dry season, races and events were held on it.

Today, the Santa Barbara water desalination treatment plant occupies part of the old El Estero location.

What's now the Andrée Clark Bird Refuge used to be the outlet for Sycamore Creek. When the creek was blocked, a stagnant pool formed in dry months. Finally in 1928 the Clark family, who owned the big estate on the nearby bluff, came forth with funds to make what had become a neglected salt pond into a true bird sanctuary. Mrs. Clark wanted to name it after Huguette's sister, Andrée.

A shallow lake was sculpted around three small islands, and seawater was originally set to flow through a dike so the area would be somewhat tidal. Over the years, the Refuge has attracted many birds. However, it badly needs a facelift, which has been scheduled to take place soon.

Until then, the Bird Refuge is subject to algae blooms due to the warm days.

Nature Journal: September 4, 2021
Andrée Clark Bird Refuge

The word was out loud and clear: come to the Bird Refuge if you can stand the smell and you'll be rewarded by shorebirds everywhere!

And who was I to hold back from that. My only problem was my caregiver, Jean, who has a very delicate sense of smell. I know she doesn't complain, but she was dreading this visit. I'd warned her.

So here we are, getting out of the car, putting me on the walker, getting out the spotting scope, camera, and binocs, not to speak of the heavy oxygen tank that must come along as well.

I see that Dave Compton and Hugh Ranson are standing down there near the water's edge, but they're far away. The "shore" has moved 4-feet farther into the lake, and the area bordering the edge of the lake is a mass of black stinky mud with bubbles of grayish foam on top. Insects of many species inhabit these rich mudflats, and as the water dries up, they're available to the shorebirds. No wonder the place is packed.

Just have a look at the shorebirds! Small scatterings of Western and Least Sandpipers and among them, a beautiful fresh juvenile Pectoral Sandpiper. The "Pec" is taller and has a set of fine brown streakings that stop abruptly just beneath its chest.

If you're standing on the "beach" near the parking lot and looking outward, you're right in the "smell tunnel," the onshore breeze is blowing toward you. Ugh! Let's walk around on the bike path to the east so we can see some of the other birds.

Fortunately, Dave Compton is walking with us, and we make it around on the bike path so now we're standing at a shady spot and looking out at the birds.

From here, I can see the way the waterline has receded all around the lake, and the muddy shores have grown wider. Shorebird heaven!

I like the chance to see the smaller of the yellowlegs, the Lesser, because it's a much more uncommon sight than our Greater Yellowlegs. Here are two young Lesser Yellowlegs hopping around in the sticky goo. They're smaller than the greater, and gluttons for flies.

And there's the American Avocet! The Avocet displays its crisp black and white plumage and feeds by swiping an up-scooped bill. The bird is in the middle of the lake, it's become that shallow.

I'm on the sidelines here, fighting with the sharp sciatic pain in my leg and cursing my back for making me hunch like an old lady. But what more can I do? Look

*at the next shorebird, that's what. And they're all here,
the Black-necked Stilts, the tiny peep.*

*To think how far these birds have come. All fall the
skies up north empty themselves of birds, birds
headed south to us here in Southern California.*

*Think of the journey. Many will go right on down to
the tip of Argentina, but most will stop somewhere
along the way, spending the winter on the temperate
shores of North or Middle America. Mudflats with food
are what keep shorebirds stoked for their migration.*

*Pondering this, I don't even smell the odor anymore!
Mind over matter? You've gotta have a lot of it.*

Fall Landbird Migration

Fall migration for landbirds is usually exciting in Santa Barbara.
We are located along the Pacific Flyway, and most birds traveling south
will be using the coast itself as a landmark. The birds are aware of the
Pacific Ocean lurking out there and they'll do everything they can to
fly over land.

And, of course, what we're really hoping to find is one of those
Eastern warblers that's become disoriented and lost. That's what the
chase-hungry birders I know want – a bird that's out of the ordinary,
doesn't belong here, and is downright rare.

Every fall is different, depending upon weather events, breeding
success of certain species, and the birding coverage we can give our
patch of southern Santa Barbara County.

Recently, trees infested with a type of sucking insect called a
"psyllid" have been a magnet for migrating songbirds. Tipuana
tipu trees form a solid canopy over a parking lot at a business park
off Hollister Avenue in Goleta. This unlikely location draws masses
of warblers. The birds eat the sugary houses that the winged
psyllid deposits.

A similar situation occurs miles away on the Riviera, where a business park harbors several large eucalyptus trees that are under attack by another kind of psyllid. Are the birds that come through just getting smarter or what? Rather than search through dry creek beds or dead foliage – typical of late summer – migrant warblers appear to seek out easy pickings like they are finding on eucalyptus leaves. And they are flocking to these two locations this fall, the places where the "psyllids" have given the birds a free lunch.

Looking back now, with some of my old journals before me, I come to the page on September 13, 2000, when I'd just found a Canada Warbler in Montecito.

I remember the day clearly: Dad had passed away many months ago, and Ellen and I had been at the family home sorting through mounds of papers, files, photos, and books. I was covered with dust and sweat. I knew the cure: a walk up Mountain Drive to refresh.

So I parked my car at the top of Riven Rock Road, and got out. And then it happened. I heard an unfamiliar call issuing from the leafy pittosporum hedge that grew on that corner.

Of course I didn't have my binocs, but I thought oh well, I'll just "pish" to see if the bird will pop up and show itself. And so I "pished," like every birder knows how to do, and up pops a bright yellow warbler with a gray back and head, and a faint dark necklace around the throat.

A Canada Warbler! A female Canada Warbler calling to me from that hedge. And that's a rare bird in Southern California.

I was thrilled. To quote from that entry: "What a spirit-lifter, day-saving, fun time it was – me all alone in the mid-afternoon sun and a Canada Warbler hops out. Travel safely, oh little one, south where you belong this winter."

Being long distance migrants, Canada Warblers have become harder to see in the intervening years, certainly scarcer in California. Their breeding territory is all across Canada; they normally migrate through the Eastern states and down into Mexico and Panama, en route to wintering in northern South America.

The coast of California isn't on their way, but that's where one landed that day in 2000.

And more recently, here's another visit from a Canada Warbler.

Nature Journal: September 19, 2021
Riviera Business Park

We're taking a chance, because there was no promise that the Canada Warbler would still be there today. But lucky for us it was seen this morning.

So we piled into the car and off we went, all my birding gear, my miracle medicine inhaler, and... I forgot... most importantly... caregiver Jean, and my friend, Carol Goodell.

I just had to see one of these rare warblers, now that we're suddenly getting the Eastern landbirds coming down the coast on a migration push. We've had a weather front, and that disturbance seems to be enough to get some of the migrating birds off course.

We arrive to a crowd of birders standing in the middle of the driveway in the Riviera business complex. What are these people doing on a quiet Sunday morning?

They're watching one of the most unpredictable shows in North America: fall migration for warblers!

I get out, grab my walker, and greet all my friends. Our birding community is caring and loving. Everyone helps me, as we get settled for the "warbler watch."

And here I am, doing what I'd never imagined: sitting in a walker looking at birds high in the eucalyptus trees! I can do it if I sit down and rest my bins on the rims of the walker. I struggle. But I'm still here.

And I finally lock my eyes on the lovely Canada Warbler, along with four or five other kinds of warblers, as they flit through the dirty-looking leaves. The leaves are "dirty" due to the lerps that have been laid down by an insect.

Somewhere along the line the birds have discovered that the diseased trees harbor snacks. Look for the "lerped eucs" and you're bound to find warblers.

From underneath, that Canada Warbler has a vibrant yellow chest, white underparts out to the base of the tail, and a slate gray back. Now, if you think you can actually see this by looking straight up at a 40-foot-high eucalyptus tree, well, it's not easy. I need time, and if I can get the spotting scope right, victory.

So I spent one of the most exciting and fulfilling Sunday mornings, reveling in the rich warblers, the peaceful Riviera setting, and the surrounding good will of birders and photographers who were all chasing the same thing I was: a chance to see a flutter of beauty from far away that had landed in Santa Barbara.

11.

New Ideas About Spring Migration

Have you ever gone online where you can see all the bird list digests from California? On May 7, 2022, I looked at the section "Southern California," then read a post that said "3,000 Western Tanagers in Gorman." Gorman?

It's a speck of buildings on the "Grapevine," that portion of Interstate 5 that winds its way through the chaparral and surrounding hillsides north out of the Los Angeles Basin.

That was the report from one birding pioneer, Richard Crossley, who happened to have bought a house in Gorman *just to find out what happens there in spring migration.*

Crazy, but true.

Crossley, a Brit, is onto something none of us native birders might ever have discovered. At dawn, he witnessed birds flying north straight into the wind as they made their way in spring migration.

These birds hugged the tails of the morning wind, whipping them along on the updraft. Also, the wind forced the birds to fly low, and as they did so they fed in a hopscotch manner, traveling through the chaparral.

And why do the birds fly *into* the wind? That's the question we're all asking and that's what Crossley discovered in his stint at Gorman.

May 12, 2022, Montecito

Over the last three nights, we've had wind, wind, wind. Mostly from the north, perhaps a little from the east, from the Santa Ana direction, meaning warming a bit.

Today, I was transfixed by the beauty of what was going on in my backyard. Western Tanagers were careening around, Black-headed Grosbeaks were at all the feeders, and Yellow Warblers came to the pond in numbers.

It's Tanager Time!

One by one they flew to the evergreen pear tree, then down to the azalea, then into the pond. The male Western Tanagers were dashing – with their red heads gleaming and black wings framing their yellow breasts. They just appear, and don't need to be pushy or throw their weight around. Those male tanagers – I love their confidence.

At the same time, I watched as a bunch of somber gray-tinged *female* Western Tanagers flew down to the pond, so quiet, tentative. There they were, just not as agile and sure of themselves as the males. They're predominantly gray in color with just a hint of yellowish-green touching their feathers. Many are juveniles from the year before, on their first journey north.

Only the lovely black-and-russet Black-headed Grosbeaks linger at the seed feeders. None of these other beauties need my feeders at all.

I kept clocking the migrants, and every time I looked up, there was a Yellow Warbler, or a Western Tanager, or a Black-headed Grosbeak. I made list totals for the short amounts of time I was sitting outside, then I'd get up and send my lists in to eBird from my phone. It was fabulous. I've had bigger migrations, but today and yesterday were the kind of days I enjoy when spring migration comes to my garden. Last year was a complete dud for my yard.

But I'm learning so much. About the wind direction. And how the birds want to fly *into* the wind. They seem to need that uplift to get them going, but it also keeps them down closer to the ground when they're flying. Otherwise, we'd never see them.

So on very clear days with no wind, the birds are too high for us to see as they go over. On windy days, the birds will fly at a lower elevation to avoid the heaviest winds.

These early morning flights are what everyone is trying to understand. Why do birds fly in the early morning? Some say that they will benefit by flying at dawn because they can see to feed as they make their way. Stopping and snatching something from a chaparral bush or a tree? I think we're still trying to figure this out.

May 13, 2022

Today was much less of a push, but there were still migrants in my garden. Straggling into the pond, one by one. I'd squint down into the shadows from up on the deck and there would be another one of those shy female tanagers. They're all gray, and somber, with a little yellowish-green coming in. The males were migrating as well, but not as many as yesterday. Same with the Yellow Warblers.

What I don't understand is why I'm not seeing Warbling Vireos and Wilson's Warblers – often the commonest birds flying north this time of year.

Watching Spring Migration

Imagine a warbler, like a Wilson's Warbler, that seeks to fly north from Mexico in order to nest in the U.S. and Canada. What path would the warbler follow? The answer: the straightest, fastest, easiest route, with some food and water along the way.

They fly over the border, cross the Mojave Desert, then head straight up the big Central Valley of California. In order to observe these flights, a birder might find a place where the flocks of migrants get funneled into a narrow passage. Usually the birds are flying into a headwind, otherwise they will be too high.

For example, in the San Gabriel Mountains, which form a barrier between the Los Angeles Basin and points north, a pass at Bear Divide acts as a major funnel. Recently, researchers and volunteers have monitored this spot by counting the birds on a daily basis in spring migration.

On certain days, if you're at the right location, the numbers of birds are massive. Trial-and-error is the name of the game when it comes to finding where the birds are going to be concentrated. People who have the ingenuity to figure it out will lead the way.

For example, in spring of 2021, the Gorman Pass area (Crossley again) reported a flock of 500 Lawrence's Goldfinches, hundreds of Ash-throated Flycatchers, thousands of White-crowned Sparrows, hundreds of kingbirds, Empidonax flycatchers, and Wilson's Warblers.

This is new information. Up to now, nobody realized the numbers of birds in spring migration at certain key spots in California. We assumed small land birds migrated only at night. This turns out not to be true, at least not in parts of California. In addition, the significance of wind direction hasn't been fully figured out.

Landbirds don't fly all night in migration, but perhaps stop pre-dawn, then get up and join a dawn flight until mid-morning. That way they can see where they're going, and perhaps snatch some food as they fly along. Nobody seems to know what happens to migrants after mid-day. They disperse throughout the landscape and become difficult to track.

And then there's the phenomenon at Mount Soledad near the San Diego coast. Here Paul Lehman, another expert birder, has observed dawn flights of birds heading into the northeast wind up over the mountain. It's not a funnel situation, but because the birds are close to the coast, they have to do this to get back on track going north. Otherwise, they're out off the ocean.

Santa Barbara's Spring Migration

Another tricky aspect comes for those of us who live along the southern California coast between Carpinteria and Gaviota. Our chances of seeing a good flight in spring depends upon winds.

Normally, we're not going to get a shot at seeing the most birds, because they'll stay away from the coast. They prefer the direct route north through the interior of the state, like at Bear Divide and Gorman.

However, especially after a low-pressure trough moves through, wind will follow. If the wind is strong enough with an easterly component, birds will be blown toward the coast. At the same time, the wind is usually coming from the north as well. These northeasterly winds are perfect for us on the south coast. Since our coastline here runs east-west, the birds are blown off course, and then must redirect themselves by flying north up the canyons. (Birds come to my yard before they've headed north.)

Birders who chose the right spots up the north-south trending canyons, such as Refugio and Romero, had a nice show of small landbirds whizzing by on their way up and over the Santa Ynez Mountains. If you were in a canyon, the wind would hold down the birds and the birds would be "riding" the uplift of that wind to go up and over.

Conclusion

I've thrown out lots of new ideas here, but this is what many birders are talking about when it comes to learning more about migration. I suspect the truth lies somewhere in between: some small birds migrate at night, some during the day. Some join dawn flights, some don't. And so forth.

Stay tuned to see how this all filters out. We'll all learn together how to discover changing migration patterns in bird populations.

12.

Living And Writing

One day I asked my father, "How do you balance the writing and the living? How do you have time to write if you're deep in the groove of living: birding, teaching, raising a family?"

He had no answer, except to smile and say, "You have to do both!"

Up to now, I didn't realize that I cannot write what I haven't felt or seen. To live is to experience the senses. In older age, these are dull or departed, so bind them to you when you are young and healthy. Sip every last bit of the living. That's what I did.

Now, at the end of my life, when I'm not so busy, and when I have written a lot about life, is there still stuff happening? How's that possible? Is there anything else, or can we scoop up the life and say "Here it is – all done now!"

Well, no you can't. It turns out there's more living to be done, and you have to be stronger than you ever were before.

Just when you think you've got it all figured out, let me suggest that you don't.

Musings on Pain

Suddenly, on July 4, 2021, I pulled a muscle that caused my back to crunch out of alignment. Due to scoliosis (spinal curvature) my back triggered a lacerating sciatic pain down my left leg. I was unable to walk. It felt like a torn hamstring, but it was all the way down my leg from my left buttock to my ankle. And it had a torque to it like a snake.

I named my sciatic nerve "the snake." This nerve has the size and importance of a major big-wig in the body.

The snake was with me day and night, and there were certain positions more comfortable than others.

And it seemed as though everyone I talked to had a sciatic pain theory.

So here I was in a new land, the land of *pain*. Pain hadn't been a companion during the lung crises. I started researching this area of discomfort and I found out how tight the regulation is on opioids, so that my doctor can't prescribe much for pain.

The doctors were straightforward as to the cure: an epidural with some sort of cortisone. That might help, they said, but "everyone's different." With a shrug of the shoulders, the doctor has spoken.

In the end I had four shots, the last one administered in January 2022. I was not expecting anything, nobody I'd talked to had got much relief from epidurals, but I had to try it.

And then, nothing. Pain continued. Pills taken. So much for that cure!

Still Some Joy

So NO. I don't know where this life is going. I am a piece of the earth that's still here, still taking joy in a delightful Thanksgiving, one where I truly gave more thanks than ever before.

Have I not lived my whole life through the depth of my experiences in nature?

Now, when I need it most, I can put the oxygen tank in my walker and "walk through the pain." Until I walk without it... which continues to happen more frequently.

I've found that no matter what, I need to exercise. In order to do so, my birding targets are places where a level path exists. Today I was out on the bluffs, following UCSB's West Campus trail toward Coal Oil Point.

The morning was filled with glorious sunshine, the ocean calm as a lake. Masses of shorebirds fed amongst kelp washed up on the beach below. I set up my spotting scope, got great views from above of many shorebirds. From Willets to Least Sandpipers and lots of species in between – some ran up and back in the waves, most foraged in the algae that was covered with tiny insects of all kinds. Beach hoppers and flies in the kelp, sand crabs buried in the wet mud, and other morsels spread out in the bounteous wet sand.

And there I was: oxygen tank, caregiver, walker, and all. Looking down from the coastal cliffs onto the beach. We made a bird list, and it was a good one. I felt full to the brim of the wonder that a day of seeing masses of birds promotes.

So I can go places and while I'm there, I'm without pain completely. Taken away by the intricacy of an ordinary November day looking at waterbirds. The simple beauty and the complicated backstory. That's what I love about nature.

The ending here: my sciatic pain is helped and I am improving.

But tomorrow it could all change.

Pain Manifesto

You would think I'd get tired of it by now. Up early, nothing to eat or drink after midnight, no blood-thinners, no NSAIDs (Aleve, Advil which I need) for three days beforehand.

So in you go, yep, for the *last* time, and hey, this time it's *got* to work, right? And the drug to help with nerve pain is a cognitive killer, so I don't want to have to rely on it. Although I do sneak some at night for sleep.

Rather than being drugged up, I'm choosing to have the pain physician go in and deaden the nerve, and/or give me a cortisone epidural. Both were on the schedule today.

It's extremely difficult to watch birds if you can't stand up straight and look out in front of you. Looking down at the ground won't do it.

And that's what I'm resorting to; looking down with my neck attached to a downward swivel, and all due to the aging process and a curved spine like mine. The curved spine swells, traps, then pinches the nerve that's leading from it, to be felt all the way to the tips of my toes on my left leg. I can't take constant pain.

But my pain doctor, I'll call him the Magic Man, is in the business. I hope he knows what he's doing. In the old days when I was hurting on the other side of my back, this doc knew how to "freeze" the end of that nerve, keeping me pain-free for at least a year at a time.

Nerve cells will grow back, that's a stumbling point. And then you have to keep on going in and zapping them again and again. But, at some point they do give up, yay for that.

Go on, throw it at me. Oxygen, loaded needles, caregivers: do I love life too much to let it go right now, or should I chuck it in? I can, you know. Any time I get tired of this. And make no mistake, I struggle daily.

Now, the big wait, to see if the shots have taken effect. Sometimes it's a delayed reaction… and you wait and wait…

Instead of hobbling around wildly on my walker, I'm forcing myself to try to take it easy and let the medicine take effect. Drip, drip, drip, expand, expand, expand, cushion, cushion, cushion. Then the nerve won't be unprotected against the bone.

Unfortunately, these darn epidurals don't have a very good track record.

Yet two months later, I find I can walk without pain again. Unaccountably, the "snake" has taken a holiday. I do not ask why or how I'm blessed with this situation. I still hobble around one-sidedly due to my spine. But the pain can be controlled with over-the-counter pills. I am incredibly grateful. I do not begin to understand the ways of aging. Why is it that one minute, I am totally consumed with one form of anguish and the next it's something else?

13.

Blackout

Fifty-seven years ago a young bride and groom were married on a stormy April 11. Water ran down the muddy hillsides and out the driveways, filling the creeks. A shower or two brought a rainbow, and we were told it was good luck to have rain on our wedding day.

Indeed, it was Gib and me, all those years ago, getting married.

And today, our anniversary, we had a fun time remembering lots of it. We went out to lunch, then came back to sit on our deck.

But it was windy out there, a chilly wind. Not a day for sitting out.

I spent much of the rest of the day writing at my desk, and keeping an eye on the highest of the eucalyptus trees. The strongest wind currents whirl those trees from side to side, even if shrubs that aren't as tall get no breeze at all.

Soon, my evening caregiver, Jean, comes to work, and we talk about the day and what she's cooking for dinner. Meanwhile the wind is getting stronger outside, and we close up the house.

Dinner is finished, and I'm at my computer when my caregiver comes to discuss her favorite topic: the oxygen tanks. She's a strong, smart woman and she doesn't feel I am emphasizing the importance of the oxygen tanks enough.

I make her sit down and tell me her main points, which are good ones. You see, we need to have a method because we have five or six large oxygen tanks and two smaller ones. All must be filled by a special machine in the garage.

I can never be without supplemental oxygen to breathe, due to my lung disease. So, either I will be outside hooked up to one of the tanks, say, if I'm going out to lunch with friends, or, if I'm inside, I'll be always hooked up to the big concentrator, which runs on electricity and keeps me going all day, because I need it.

And then, while I'm in the middle of a sentence, PFFFT all the lights go off. The concentrator lets out a long BEEP, and the house lies quiet and dark.

Of course, we're used to this. Living in Southern California, the wind is always a problem when it comes to electric power. So many times we've fallen asleep by candle light, or flashlights.

But that was before I got sick.

I immediately go lie down on my bed and think what I should do, while I connect to a portable oxygen tank.

Meanwhile, poor Gib and Jean are outside trying to figure out who has power on our street. For some reason, the north part of the street always has power when the southern part doesn't. Our street is on two separate grids.

We look over and see that our neighbor, Debbie Branch, a long-time friend and a widow who lives on her own, has her *lights on*! Thank goodness.

But Gib insists on trying to run our generator, which ends up noisy and full of fumes. The gas in it lasts about 15 minutes, then the big oxygen machine goes dead.

I can feel the panic rising inside me, but I just lie there. What can I do? This is the night we've always dreaded, ever since I got this disease. And guess what? We never worked it out. We were afraid. We didn't want to know how big a problem it was.

Jean saved me by packing up a little bag with all my medications, and other things I'd need for the night. Then we made our way over to Debbie Branch's house. Poor thing, don't think she was really expecting a night visitor, but here was Gib with the big concentrator oxygen machine on a dolly, and me trailing behind.

We all had big flashlights, but we had no idea what we should be doing. I'd called Southern California Edison Company, as had Gib, and they said it was a eucalyptus tree downed. Estimated time for reliable power on our grid was several hours from now.

There was no choice for me.

I had to sleep on Debbie's living room couch if I wanted to make it through the night. What would I have done without Debbie?

Gib went back over to our house to keep our dog, Bud, company. Debbie has a cat, who would not have taken kindly to Bud.

The wind whipped around the corners and whooshed up the street. It was a typical, cold Santa Ana wind.

I snuggled up to my green oxygen cord, put on my mask, and there I was, cozy and comfortable hooked up to my big oxygen machine, plugged in at somebody else's house. All night long.

I guess we all awoke at about six. Gib came over and said he'd driven to the corner of Olive Mill and Hot Springs Road where the tree was down. The men there told him two or three hours and it would be fixed. All night long one tree had done that much damage! Later, I drove by the tree, and I could see that if it was interwoven with wires it might take a long time to unravel. But 12 hours?

Yep, that's what it was: 12 hours of darkness and no heat, no stove, no light, and *no oxygen*!

What am I going to do next time? That's all I can think of now.

We need to research a variety of ways, but all of them are expensive. Portable ways of carrying power around don't come cheap.

Our anniversary, these 57 years.

As I walked with my walker up Pimiento Lane in the warm evening sun, I stopped when I saw Myron Shapiro, another neighbor. His philosophy is that it's good for us to be put off balance a bit, and for things to not be quite right. He says it helps us grow and deal with the ups and downs of life.

At 8:30 a.m., when we got the call that power had been restored, I wasn't thinking of exercising my psyche. But he may have a point.

He's a doctor to the rich and famous in Beverly Hills, and he must know what he's talking about.

He pronounced it wonderful to have challenges, because how we react to them is good for us. Stretches us out. Makes us change course, go up, down, or sideways.

Several weeks later, a very large package arrived that contained a battery charger that will last us for over 10 hours. All we do is plug in my big concentrator, and I'm good for that amount of oxygen. No more worries when the power goes out.

⤞☙⟡❧⤝

That was my anniversary celebration 57 years on. Something tells me that if I am even alive for the next one, it may be pretty dull in comparison.

14.

A Monster In My Bedroom

After my last visit to my pulmonologist, I knew I was in for trouble.

And when a man in a dark uniform and a mask (we're all still in masks these days from the pandemic) came to my front door, I knew the trouble was starting sooner than I'd expected.

At my recent appointment, the doctor said that when they measured the carbon dioxide in my arteries, it was too high.

However, he was quite excited, as he always is, at the prospect of using a *new machine*.

Oh no.

"But wait till you see this, Joan," and he made it sound like nothing more than a CPAP attachment that so many folks use these days for irregular breathing at night. A mask. Well, I'm okay with a mask.

But what I saw was something else.

The man at my front door set up this ominous-looking gizmo in my bedroom, which took him over an hour to install.

Then he showed me how it was supposed to work.

I thought to myself, I *cannot* do this.

The machine is a mini-ventilator that's supposed to help me breathe at night so I'll get rid of the carbon dioxide in my system. It helps my heart get rid of extra water I might retain, too.

The resemblance to a mini-computer means that someone, somewhere, can see how long I've been on the device and what has happened during that time. So I have to "turn on and off" the screen on this devilish black thing.

I wouldn't mind it so much if the device didn't *beep* constantly at me whenever the slightest thing goes wrong. I'm learning to ignore the frightening alarm beeps, but I'm never going to be able to sleep with this setup.

Furthermore, there's an extended coil that fits tightly into a mask, which fits tightly over my face. I am strapped in like a spaceman.

How am I supposed to put my oxygen tube in and out of this thing if I need to have a snack or go to the bathroom at night? The guy looked at me in shock. "Oh, you have to get up in the night?"

Gib gets home tomorrow and I'm waiting for his wise advice on how to deal with this machine. The caregivers will help me, I'm sure.

Depressing to know that I need to take further steps down the road, so to speak.

But I know that my wonder nebulizer medicine isn't as good as it once was, doesn't last as long as it used to, and I run out of energy more quickly than before.

If it's CO_2, that's one thing. But if I have to incur sleepless nights of suffocation and worry – well, I'll just have to decide.

Gib has been gone this week, and it's been a time for me to discover how lonely it is without one's mate. I'm not lonely for people, I have plenty of them around and have all week. But I'm lonely for someone I can talk to about myself, my reading, and the events of my life.

⤙❦⤚

Now it's Tuesday, and the man with the mask has come and gone. Gib was here, thank God, and was able to see how it's going to work. I have an open strap that comes over my head, ending up under my chin with two magnets to hold it together. The mask itself is a tight fit right around my mouth and nose. The trick is to get off the big cannula that brings oxygen from my tank and quickly put it into this new machine, turn the machine on, then put the head gear on, and it should start automatically, breathing with my breaths.

That's after I remember to take out my barrette, my hearing aids, take off my glasses – but keep them nearby so I can see the screen.

The point is, I have to be pretty much settled into one position because I don't have much leeway to move around.

Is this just another extender that will eventually fail me? I'm afraid it is. But I guess I'm alright with buying some more time, am I not?

The one good thing is that I have ankles again. Yes, the elephantine ankles have disappeared, becoming those of a gazelle. The new breathing machine is responsible for that, and I'm so grateful. I can take a day or two off from the support stockings.

If I can do the mini-ventilator on my terms, this might work. It definitely fills the gaps between the miracle inhaler, which can't shoulder all the breathing by itself anymore.

Four visits later, and I may be able to manage the new monster. A very caring and patient employee at Super Care has been my savior, explaining everything over and over to me and to Gib. First off, he gave me a new, smaller mask to work with. And now I understand that he has set the alarms to a quiet tone, so as to interrupt my sleep as little as possible.

I'm going to try to be positive, because I must rid my body of this awful CO_2, the carbon dioxide that slows me down and makes me tired.

Epilogue

I have to be an example to people now. Everyone is watching, can she do it? Can she go on living and be a viable person? Can she keep and be a force in a conversation.

I am so lucky to have a spirit that wants to be here and that's surrounded by life and fun. When you lose the inside sense of fun and drama, it's gone. You must keep the laughing and the funny little asides up and running, see the craziness of it all.

It's not that simple, however. Old age is working on my body. I defeat one ailment, another pops up. Surrounding myself with beauty and nature, family and loved ones, is the only lasting cure.

I relish my grandchildren, Alex and Annabel. The joy of being with young people is a supreme comfort.

><⊷∙∙✦∙∙⊷><

Youth is NOT wasted on the young.

I remember the happiness I felt when I was a young woman, back home from college for the summer. Once again, I had returned to "my place," my Santa Barbara.

It's filled with the birds and animals I love, the land that I cling to, the familiar smells of the sandy shore, the chaparral, and the high mountains.

I was going over to see an old girlfriend from high school, driving the beige Ford that grandmother Nin had given us.

I would've been at the beach all day, and my tan legs were displayed under cut-off jeans – at a modest length in those days. And a white T-shirt or simple blouse completed the outfit. Sandals or tennis shoes on my feet.

The memories are clear. I am young, feel hopeful and joyous. I look at the Santa Ynez Mountains fading into twilight and my heart jumps. That's the connection with a pile of sandstone rock, a landmark I can never forget.

Then I said to myself: Remember you are young and you're happy, you aren't in pain and you're very lucky. And I felt the intensity of it all, perhaps a hint of what life might bring, how different it would be from anything I imagined. I knew I could do it. I was in an outburst of love and joy, at my surroundings, at my life. Not that it had been that exciting up to then, but I was happy. And I had an inkling then that being in nature in "my place" had something to do with it.

I'd just seen the Great Horned Owl perched on the wire up on Mountain Drive while I was taking an evening walk, I'd just learned that the huffing sound coming from the eucalyptus grove across the street was a Band-tailed Pigeon. I was filled with these little discoveries and whatever else I could find on my own.

At the same time, I was a college sophomore, still in the mix of that kind of fun, still taking part in all of what I'd call the normal universe.

But that evening, as I settled in to drive to my girlfriend's house, something touched me. My gratitude for this good life overran my college brain, leaving a glimpse of that other world I'd enjoyed in bits and pieces as a child. I want it back now, I thought to myself.

I am full up with life and the promises it holds. Bring it on, because I'm ready for the challenge.

And I could say this because in the first place I was born with a happy disposition like my mother, and in the second, I saw through a tiny crack where I might go with my early ties to Santa Barbara.

Where I might go with my fascination for birds, a passion that I had put aside for awhile, but one that would not be quelled.

Don't tell me youth is wasted on the young. I was present at every moment of my life. Young emotions are especially strong, and I clearly had those feelings of being young and being happy and knowing it might change. But to me, if I had my world of nature around me as my touchstone, I was okay.

The other aspect of my future was when I met Gib. He gave me the confidence to be absolutely my true self. He was proud of my birding interests. He recognized it was unusual, but he urged me to pursue my passion. I wouldn't realize that until later.

And I felt increasingly well and vigorous as I went through high school and college. I had energy for everything, and I kept that throughout most of my adult life.

When I was young, I gathered up all of life's good things, because it was then that every part of my body worked and I knew it might not last.

Acknowledgments

I want to thank all the dear friends who helped me on this journey. The birding community has been wonderful. Other friends have brought food and company, which is essential to staying well.

Thanks to Marilyn Harding for acting as my chauffeur on many a birding trip.

Thanks to my sister, Ellen, for her encouragement and my daughter, Jenny, for being here.

I am grateful for excellent doctors and loyal caregivers. And I am blessed with two grandchildren whom I adore.

After 57 years, Gib and I can still have fun together. I couldn't have written this book without his strong support.

Joan Easton Lentz
October 2022.

www.ingramcontent.com/pod-product-compliance
Lightning Source LLC
Chambersburg PA
CBHW022340280326
41934CB00006B/711